THE ROUTLEDGE ATLAS OF CLASSICAL HISTORY

THE ROUTLEDGE ATLAS OF
CLASSICAL HISTORY

Fifth edition

Michael Grant

London

First published as *The Dent Atlas of Classical History* 1971 by J M Dent

Fifth edition published 1994 by Routledge
11 New Fetter Lane, London EC4P 4EE

© 1971, 1974, 1986, 1989, 1994 Michael Grant Publications Ltd

Printed and bound in Great Britain by
Butler & Tanner Ltd, Frome and London

British Library Cataloguing in Publication Data
A catalogue record for this book is available from the British Library.

ISBN 0–415–11934–0 (hbk)
ISBN 0–415–11935–9 (pbk)

Preface

This is an atlas of the classical world – the ancient Greek and Roman world, which needs to be understood if we are to understand the world of today. To say that such an atlas could ever be a substitute for a historical survey would be an exaggeration. Nevertheless, geography is such a vital, indeed predominant, factor in ancient history – and such a difficult factor because of all the changes of names[1] – that the whole course of events often seems to mean practically nothing without maps, and without a lot of them, carefully devised.

Older classical atlases, apart from a varying degree of emphasis on physical aspects, tended to concentrate on political themes, and it is true enough that these stand in great need of maps. But the present volume attempts to cast the net wider, and to introduce economic, cultural, religious and other topics as well. There are also a number of town plans.

Modern research in archaeology and other fields has shown that the classical world cannot be grasped without some appreciation of what went before it. I have consequently started this book with a number of maps illustrating the Mediterranean world during the second millennium BC, and particularly during the period from 1700 BC onwards, when the international scene had already assumed a well-defined and complex appearance; and the story is carried onwards to offer brief illustrations of the Old Testament. At the other end of the story, the traditional terminal date of the ancient world, the year AD 476 when the last western emperor ceased to reign, is again not a very meaningful landmark, so I have carried on the tale until the reign of Justinian in the following century.

It will clear enough what a very great deal is owed to the talent of Arthur Banks for transcribing the written and spoken world into cartographic form. I am also most grateful to Julian Shuckburgh and Benjamin Buchan for all the assistance they rendered on behalf of the publishers, and I want to thank Jane Dorner for assistance with the index and C. R. B. Elliott for help with an earlier revised edition. Finally, I have to acknowledge a substantial debt to existing classical atlases, German and English. And I must single out, for a special word of gratitude, the *Atlas of the Classical World* edited by A. A. M. van der Heyden and H. H. Scullard for Messrs Nelson, and *Westermanns Grosser Atlas zur Weltgeschichte* (Westermann, Braunschweig). N. G. L. Hammond's *Atlas of the Greek and Roman World in Antiquity* (Noyes Press, Park Ridge) is now fundamental; so is Routledge's new classical atlas.

For this fifth edition I have added new maps on the changing frontier of the Roman Empire (maps 72 and 73), on the persecution of the Christians (map 86) and on the Roman Empire in its final years (maps 88 and 90).

1994   MICHAEL GRANT

[1] Modern names are given after the ancient in the Index.

List of Maps

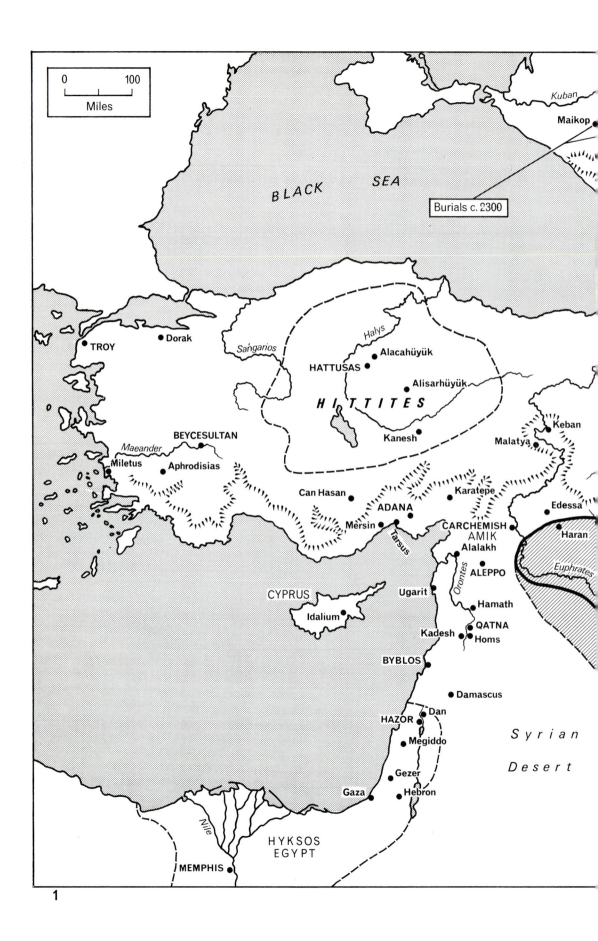

Miles

0   100

Kuban

Maikop

Burials c. 2300

BLACK   SEA

Halys

TROY

Dorak

Sangarios

Alacahüyük

HATTUSAS

Alisarhüyük

H I T T I T E S

Keban

BEYCESULTAN

Maeander

Kanesh

Malatya

Miletus

Aphrodisias

Can Hasan

Karatepe

Edessa

ADANA

Mersin

CARCHEMISH

Haran

Tarsus

AMIK

Euphrates

Alalakh

ALEPPO

CYPRUS

Ugarit

Hamath

Idalium

QATNA

Kadesh

Homs

BYBLOS

Damascus

S y r i a n

Dan

HAZOR

D e s e r t

Megiddo

Gezer

Gaza

Hebron

Nile

HYKSOS EGYPT

MEMPHIS

1

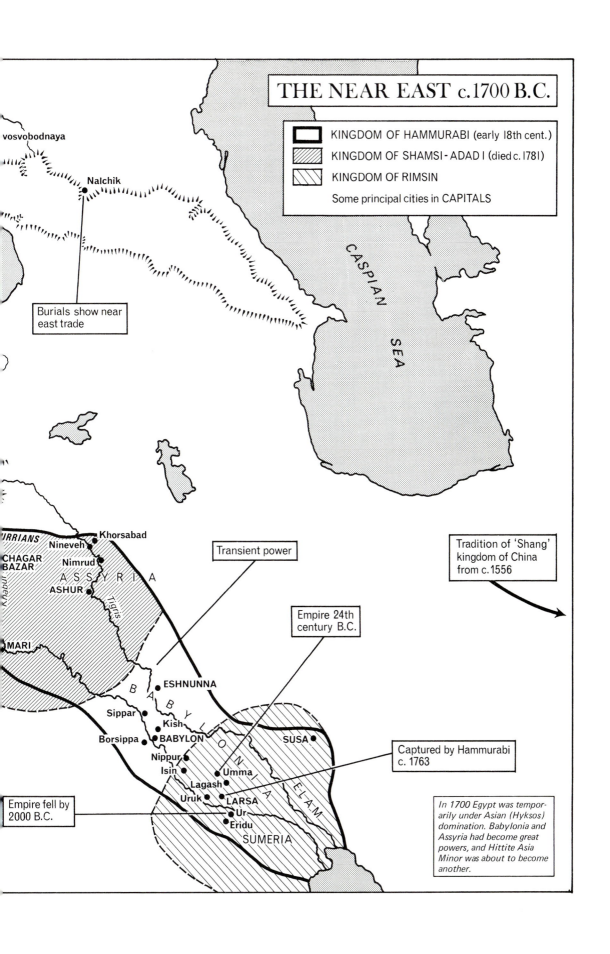

THE NEAR EAST c.1700 B.C.

◻ KINGDOM OF HAMMURABI (early 18th cent.)

▨ KINGDOM OF SHAMSI - ADAD I (died c.1781)

▨ KINGDOM OF RIMSIN

Some principal cities in CAPITALS

vosvobodnaya

Nalchik

Burials show near east trade

CASPIAN SEA

IRRIANS

Nineveh

Khorsabad

CHAGAR BAZAR

Nimrud

ASSYRIA

ASHUR

MARI

Tigris

Khabur

Tradition of 'Shang' kingdom of China from c.1556

Transient power

Empire 24th century B.C.

ESHNUNNA

BABYLONIA

Sippar

Kish

Borsippa

BABYLON

SUSA

Captured by Hammurabi c. 1763

Nippur

Isin

Umma

ELAM

Empire fell by 2000 B.C.

Lagash

Uruk

LARSA

Ur

Eridu

SUMERIA

In 1700 Egypt was temporarily under Asian (Hyksos) domination. Babylonia and Assyria had become great powers, and Hittite Asia Minor was about to become another.

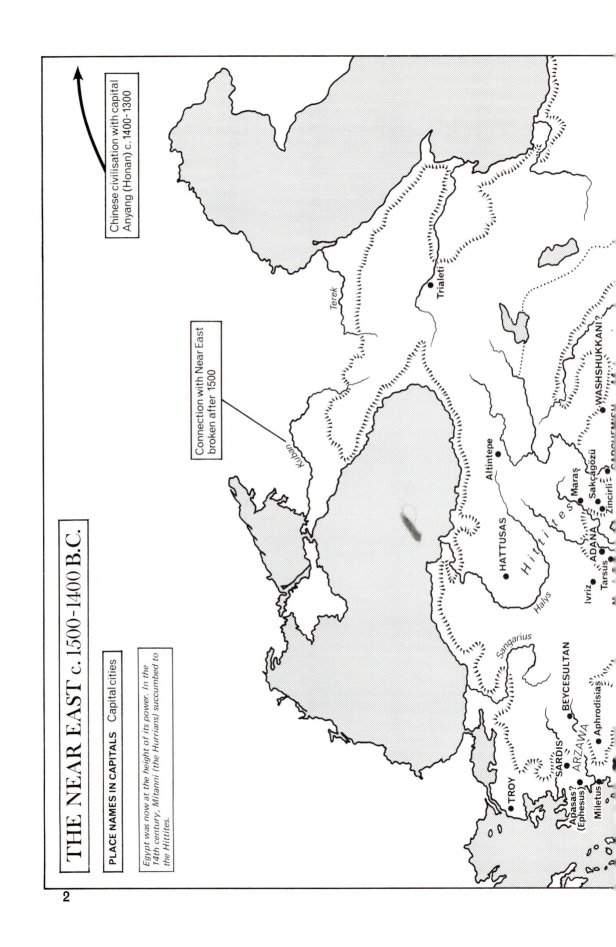

THE NEAR EAST c. 1500-1400 B.C.

PLACE NAMES IN CAPITALS Capital cities

Egypt was now at the height of its power. In the 14th century, Mitanni (the Hurrians) succumbed to the Hittites.

Chinese civilisation with capital Anyang (Honan) c. 1400-1300

Connection with Near East broken after 1500

Terek

Kuban

Trialeti

Altintepe

WASHSHUKKANI?

Maraş

Sakçagözü

Zincirli

HATTUSAS

H i t t i t e s

ADANA

Ivriz

Tarsus

Halys

Sangarius

BEYCESULTAN

SARDIS

ARZAWA

Aphrodisias

TROY

Apasas? (Ephesus)

Miletus

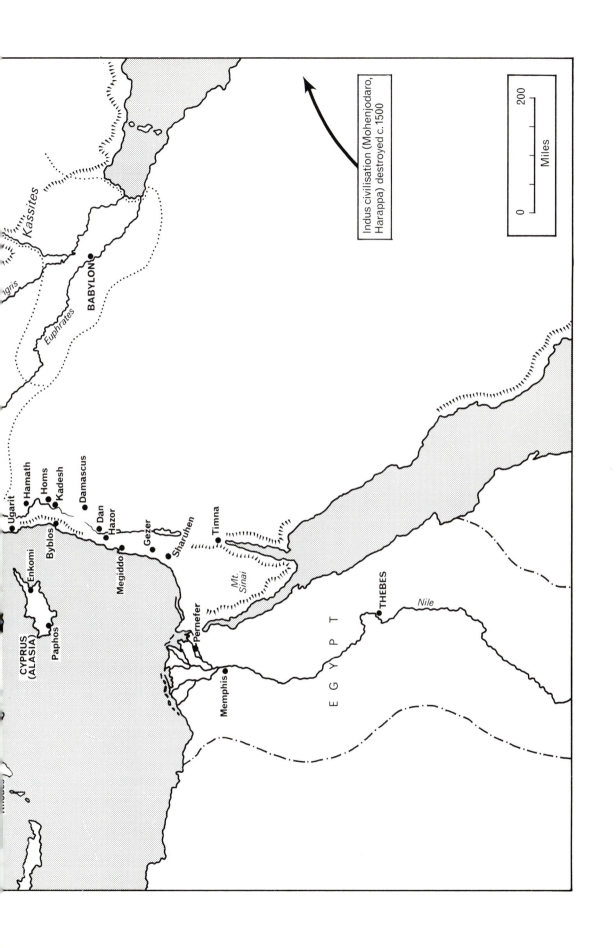

Indus civilisation (Mohenjodaro, Harappa) destroyed c. 1500

0   200
Miles

Kassites

Tigris

Euphrates

BABYLON

Ugarit
Hamath
Homs
Kadesh
Damascus
Byblos
Dan
Hazor
Gezer
Sharuhen
Timna
Enkomi
Megiddo
Mt. Sinai

CYPRUS
(ALASIA)
Paphos

Pernefer

E G Y P T

THEBES
Nile

Memphis

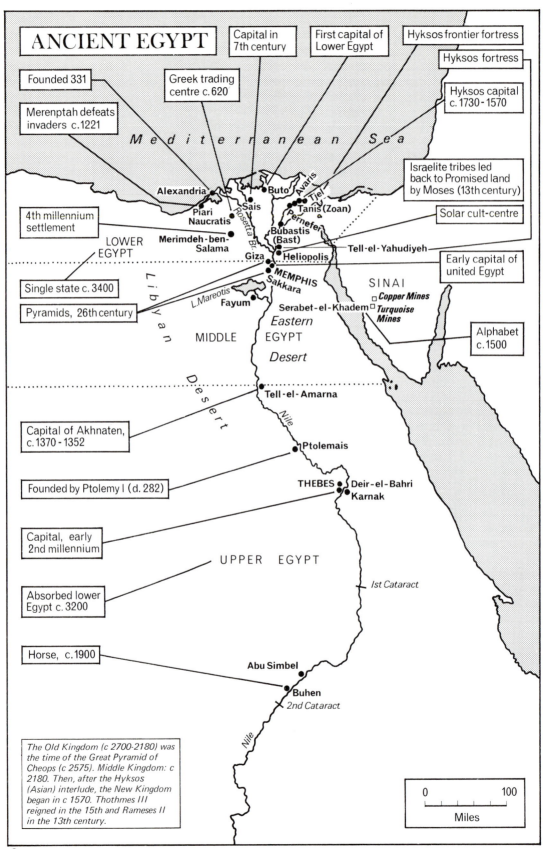

ANCIENT EGYPT

Capital in 7th century

First capital of Lower Egypt

Hyksos frontier fortress

Hyksos fortress

Founded 331

Greek trading centre c.620

Hyksos capital c.1730-1570

Merenptah defeats invaders c.1221

Israelite tribes led back to Promised land by Moses (13th century)

4th millennium settlement

Solar cult-centre

Mediterranean Sea

Alexandria

Buto

Avaris

Tiel

Sais

Pernefer

Piari
Naucratis

Tanis (Zoan)

Bubastis (Bast)

Merimdeh-ben-Salama

Tell-el-Yahudiyeh

Giza

Heliopolis

Early capital of united Egypt

LOWER EGYPT

Rosetta Br.

Single state c.3400

MEMPHIS
Sakkara

S I N A I

□ **Copper Mines**

L.Mareotis

Fayum

Pyramids, 26th century

L i b y a n

Serabet-el-Khadem □ **Turquoise Mines**

Eastern EGYPT Desert

MIDDLE

Alphabet c.1500

D e s e r t

Tell-el-Amarna

Capital of Akhnaten, c.1370-1352

Nile

Ptolemais

Founded by Ptolemy I (d. 282)

THEBES ● **Deir-el-Bahri**
Karnak

Capital, early 2nd millennium

UPPER EGYPT

1st Cataract

Absorbed lower Egypt c.3200

Horse, c.1900

Abu Simbel

Buhen
2nd Cataract

Nile

The Old Kingdom (c 2700-2180) was the time of the Great Pyramid of Cheops (c 2575). Middle Kingdom: c 2180. Then, after the Hyksos (Asian) interlude, the New Kingdom began in c 1570. Thothmes III reigned in the 15th and Rameses II in the 13th century.

0   100

Miles

3

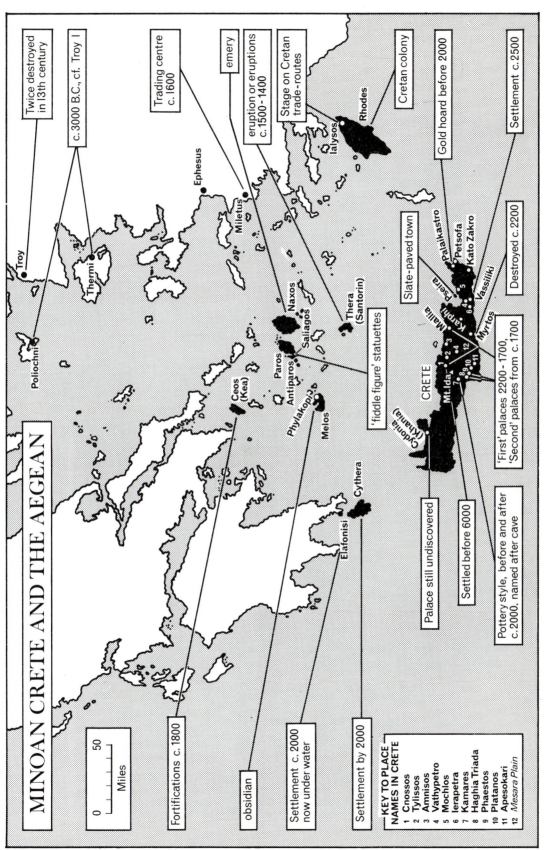

MINOAN CRETE AND THE AEGEAN

0   50

Miles

Twice destroyed in 13th century

c. 3000 B.C., cf. Troy I

Trading centre c. 1600

emery

eruption or eruptions c. 1500 – 1400

Stage on Cretan trade-routes

Cretan colony

Gold hoard before 2000

Settlement c. 2500

Troy

Poliochni

Thermi

Ephesus

Miletus

Ialysos

Rhodes

Naxos

Paros

Antiparos

Saliagos

Phylakopi

Melos

Ceos (Kea)

Thera (Santorin)

'fiddle figure' statuettes

Cythera

Elafonisi

Palaikastro

Petsofa

Kato Zakro

Vassiliki

Mallia

Pseira

Karphi

Myrtos

CRETE

Mt. Ida

Cydonia (Khania)

Slate-paved town

Destroyed c.2200

'First' palaces 2200 – 1700, 'Second' palaces from c.1700

Pottery style, before and after c.2000, named after cave

Settled before 6000

Palace still undiscovered

Fortifications c.1800

obsidian

Settlement c. 2000 now under water

Settlement by 2000

KEY TO PLACE
NAMES IN CRETE
1 Cnossos
2 Tylissos
3 Amnisos
4 Vathypetro
5 Mochlos
6 Ierapetra
7 Kamares
8 Haghia Triada
9 Phaestos
10 Platanos
11 Apesokari
12 *Mesara Plain*

4

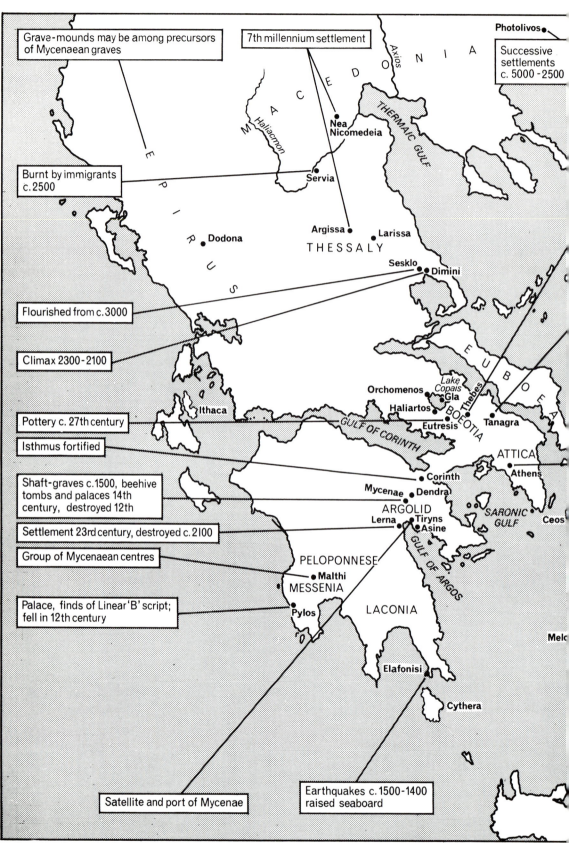

Grave-mounds may be among precursors of Mycenaean graves

7th millennium settlement

Successive settlements c. 5000-2500

Photolivos

Burnt by immigrants c. 2500

Flourished from c. 3000

Climax 2300-2100

Pottery c. 27th century

Isthmus fortified

Shaft-graves c.1500, beehive tombs and palaces 14th century, destroyed 12th

Settlement 23rd century, destroyed c. 2100

Group of Mycenaean centres

Palace, finds of Linear 'B' script; fell in 12th century

Satellite and port of Mycenae

Earthquakes c. 1500-1400 raised seaboard

Axios

MACEDONIA

THERMAIC GULF

Haliacmon

Nea Nicomedeia

Servia

Dodona

Argissa

Larissa

THESSALY

Sesklo

Dimini

EPIRUS

Ithaca

Orchomenos

Lake Copais

Gla

Thebes

Haliartos

BOEOTIA

Eutresis

Tanagra

EUBOEA

GULF OF CORINTH

ATTICA

Athens

Corinth

Mycenae

Dendra

ARGOLID

SARONIC GULF

Ceos

Lerna

Tiryns

Asine

PELOPONNESE

GULF OF ARGOS

Malthi

MESSENIA

LACONIA

Pylos

Melo

Elafonisi

Cythera

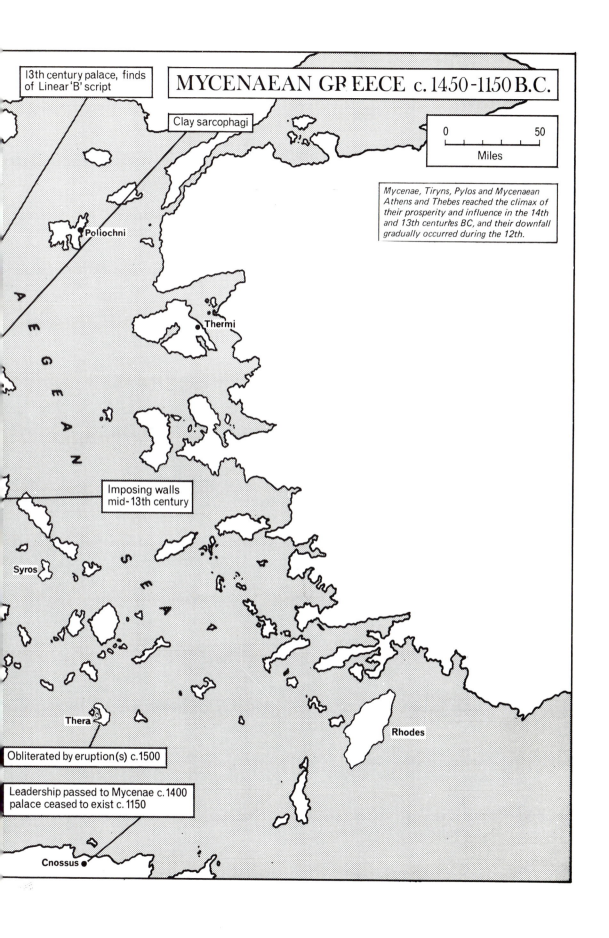

MYCENAEAN GREECE c. 1450-1150 B.C.

13th century palace, finds
of Linear 'B' script

Clay sarcophagi

0   50
Miles

*Mycenae, Tiryns, Pylos and Mycenaean
Athens and Thebes reached the climax of
their prosperity and influence in the 14th
and 13th centuries BC, and their downfall
gradually occurred during the 12th.*

Poliochni

A
E
G
E
A
N

Thermi

Imposing walls
mid-13th century

A
E
G
E
A
N

S
E
A

Syros

Thera

Rhodes

Obliterated by eruption(s) c.1500

Leadership passed to Mycenae c.1400
palace ceased to exist c.1150

Cnossus

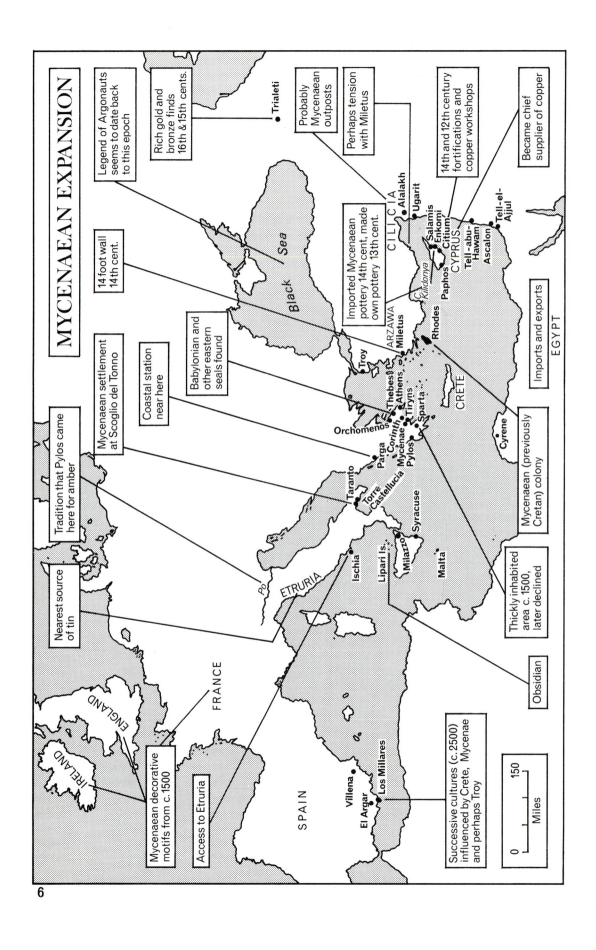

MYCENAEAN EXPANSION

Legend of Argonauts seems to date back to this epoch

Rich gold and bronze finds 16th & 15th cents.

Probably Mycenaean outposts

Perhaps tension with Miletus

14th and 12th century fortifications and copper workshops

Became chief supplier of copper

14 foot wall 14th cent.

Imported Mycenaean pottery 14th cent, made own pottery 13th cent.

Babylonian and other eastern seals found

Mycenaean settlement at Scoglio del Tonno

Coastal station near here

Tradition that Pylos came here for amber

Nearest source of tin

Mycenaean decorative motifs from c.1500

Access to Etruria

Mycenaean (previously Cretan) colony

Thickly inhabited area c. 1500, later declined

Obsidian

Imports and exports

Successive cultures (c.2500) influenced by Crete, Mycenae and perhaps Troy

Black Sea

Trialeti

CILICIA

Alalakh

Ugarit

Salamis

Enkomi

Citium

CYPRUS

Tell-el-Ajiul

Tell-abu-Hawam

Ascalon

Paphos

C. *Klidonya*

Rhodes

ARZAWA

Miletus

Troy

Thebes

Athens

Orchomenos

Corinth

Tiryns

Mycenae

Sparta

Pylos

Parga

CRETE

Cyrene

Taranto

Torre Castellucia

Syracuse

Malta

Milazzo

Lipari Is.

Ischia

ETRURIA

Po

FRANCE

ENGLAND

IRELAND

SPAIN

Villena

El Argar

Los Millares

EGYPT

0   150

Miles

6

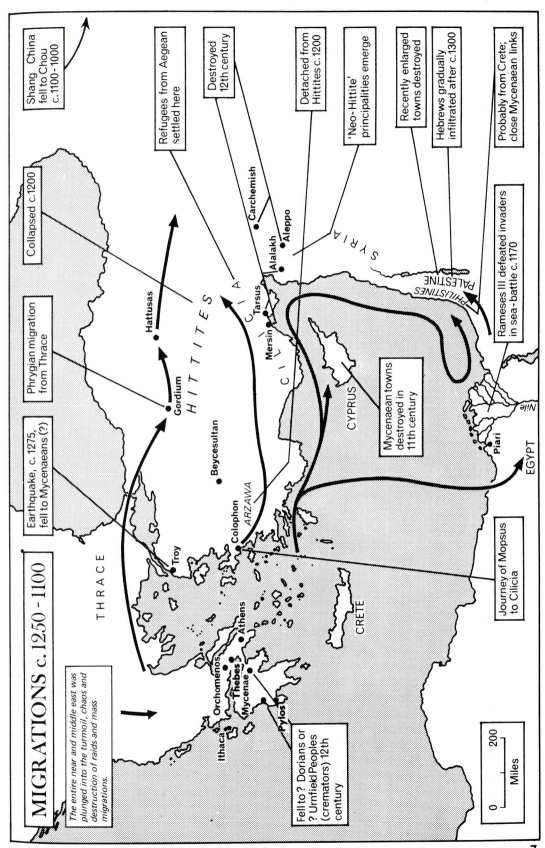

MIGRATIONS c. 1250 – 1100

The entire near and middle east was plunged into the turmoil, chaos and destruction of raids and mass migrations.

Shang China fell to Chou c. 1100 - 1000

Refugees from Aegean settled here

Destroyed 12th century

Detached from Hittites c. 1200

'Neo-Hittite' principalities emerge

Recently enlarged towns destroyed

Hebrews gradually infiltrated after c. 1300

Probably from Crete; close Mycenaean links

Rameses III defeated invaders in sea-battle c. 1170

Collapsed c. 1200

Phrygian migration from Thrace

Earthquake, c. 1275, fell to Mycenaeans (?)

Mycenaean towns destroyed in 11th century

Journey of Mopsus to Cilicia

Fell to ? Dorians or ? Urnfield Peoples (cremators) 12th century

Carchemish

Aleppo

Alalakh

SYRIA

Tarsus

Mersin

CILICIA

PALESTINE

PHILISTINES

Nile

EGYPT

Piari

CYPRUS

Hattusas

HITTITES

Gordium

Beycesultan

Colophon

ARZAWA

Troy

THRACE

Athens

Orchomenos

Thebes

Mycenae

Ithaca

Pylos

CRETE

0   200
Miles

7

PHOENICIAN TRADE & COLONISATION

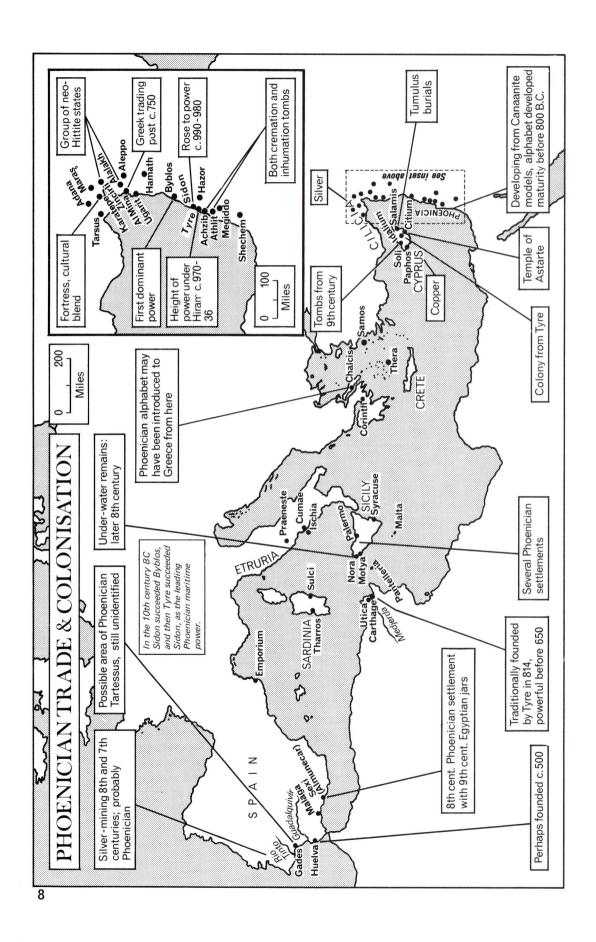

Silver-mining 8th and 7th centuries; probably Phoenician

Possible area of Phoenician Tartessus, still unidentified

Under-water remains: later 8th century

Phoenician alphabet may have been introduced to Greece from here

In the 10th century BC Sidon succeeded Byblos, and then Tyre succeeded Sidon, as the leading Phoenician maritime power.

Perhaps founded c.500

8th cent. Phoenician settlement with 9th cent. Egyptian jars

Traditionally founded by Tyre in 814, powerful before 650

Several Phoenician settlements

Colony from Tyre

Copper

Temple of Astarte

Developing from Canaanite models, alphabet developed maturity before 800 B.C.

Tumulus burials

Silver

Tombs from 9th century

Both cremation and inhumation tombs

Rose to power c. 990 – 980

Greek trading post c.750

Group of neo-Hittite states

Fortress, cultural blend

First dominant power

Height of power under Hiram c. 970 – 36

Inset map labels
Adana
Maras
Aleppo
Tarsus
Karatepe
Alalakh
Al Mina
Ugarit
Hamath
Byblos
Sidon
Tyre
Achzib
Hazor
Athlit
Megiddo
Shechem

0   100
Miles

Main map labels
SPAIN
RIO TINTO
Gades
Huelva
Guadalquivir
Malaga
Sexi (Almunecar)
Emporium
SARDINIA
Tharros
Sulci
Nora
Motya
Utica
Carthage
Pantelleria
Medjerda
ETRURIA
Praeneste
Cumae
Ischia
Palermo
SICILY
Syracuse
Malta
Chalcis
Samos
Corinth
Thera
CRETE
CILICIA
Soli
Salamis
Paphos
Citium
CYPRUS
PHOENICIA
See inset above

0   200
Miles

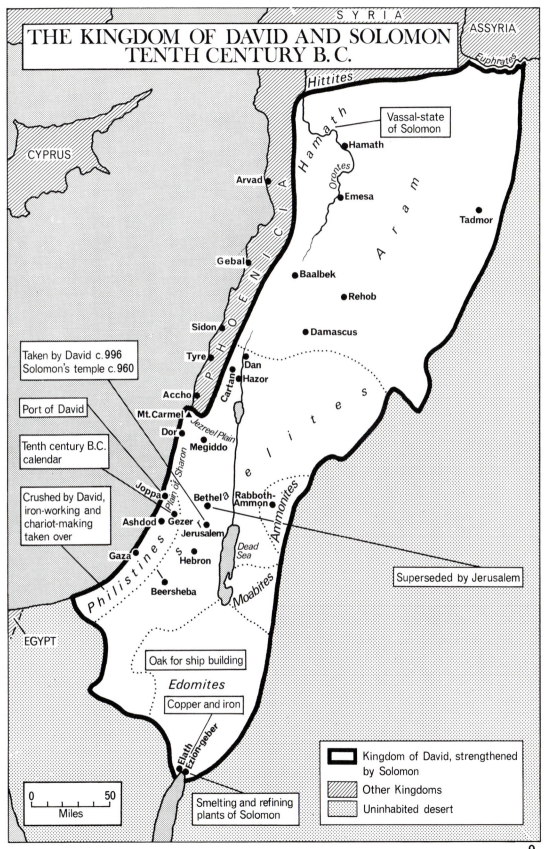

THE KINGDOM OF DAVID AND SOLOMON TENTH CENTURY B.C.

SYRIA

ASSYRIA

Euphrates

Hittites

CYPRUS

Hamath

Vassal-state of Solomon

Hamath

Arvad

Orontes

Emesa

Tadmor

Aram

Gebal

Baalbek

Rehob

Sidon

Damascus

Tyre

Dan

Taken by David c. 996
Solomon's temple c. 960

Cartan

Hazor

Accho

Port of David

Mt. Carmel

Dor

Jezreel Plain

Tenth century B.C.
calendar

Megiddo

e   l   i   t   e   s

Joppa

Crushed by David,
iron-working and
chariot-making
taken over

Bethel

Rabboth-
Ammon

Ashdod

Gezer

Ammonites

Jerusalem

Superseded by Jerusalem

Gaza

Hebron

Dead
Sea

Beersheba

Moabites

EGYPT

Oak for ship building

Edomites

Copper and iron

Elath
Ezion-geber

Kingdom of David, strengthened
by Solomon

Other Kingdoms

Uninhabited desert

0   50
Miles

Smelting and refining
plants of Solomon

9

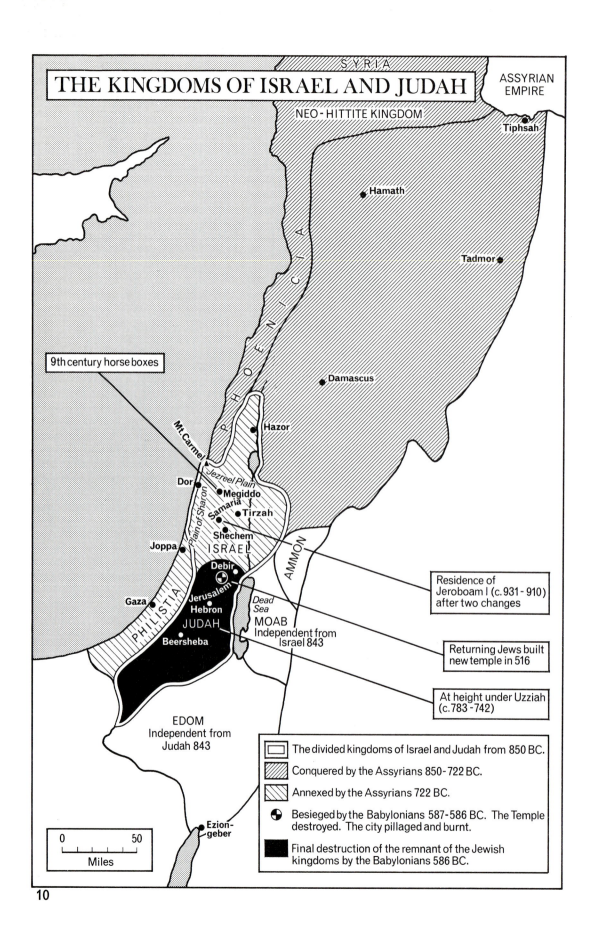

THE KINGDOMS OF ISRAEL AND JUDAH

SYRIA

ASSYRIAN EMPIRE

NEO - HITTITE KINGDOM

Tiphsah

Hamath

Tadmor

9th century horse boxes

Damascus

Mt.Carmel

Hazor

Jezreel Plain

Dor

Megiddo

Samaria

Tirzah

Shechem

Joppa

ISRAEL

AMMON

Plain of Sharon

Debir

Jerusalem

Hebron

Gaza

Dead Sea

MOAB
Independent from
Israel 843

JUDAH

Beersheba

PHILISTIA

Residence of
Jeroboam I (c. 931 - 910)
after two changes

Returning Jews built
new temple in 516

At height under Uzziah
(c. 783 - 742)

EDOM
Independent from
Judah 843

Ezion-
geber

☐	The divided kingdoms of Israel and Judah from 850 BC.
▨	Conquered by the Assyrians 850 - 722 BC.
▨	Annexed by the Assyrians 722 BC.
◑	Besieged by the Babylonians 587 - 586 BC. The Temple destroyed. The city pillaged and burnt.
■	Final destruction of the remnant of the Jewish kingdoms by the Babylonians 586 BC.

0   50
Miles

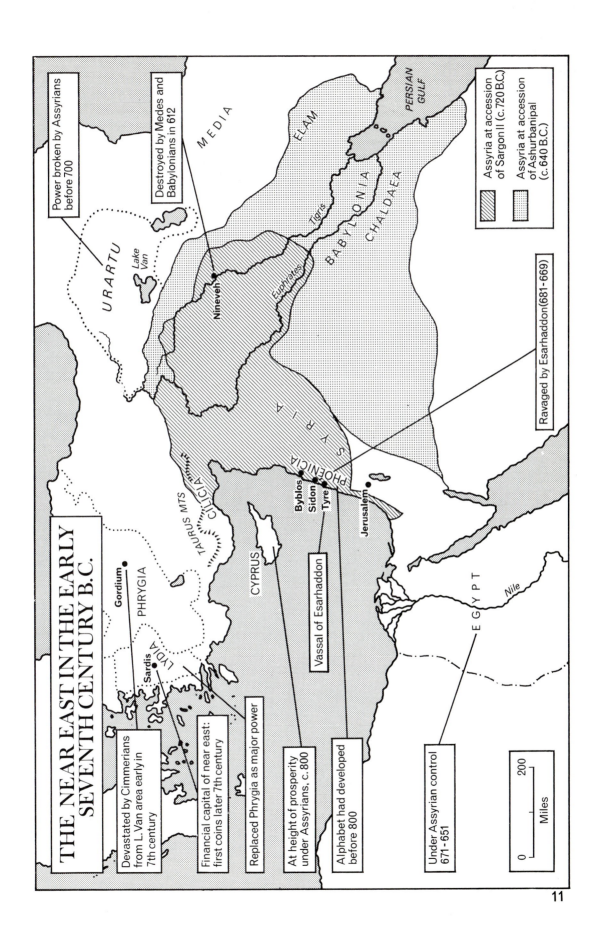

THE NEAR EAST IN THE EARLY SEVENTH CENTURY B.C.

Devastated by Cimmerians from L. Van area early in 7th century

Financial capital of near east: first coins later 7th century

Replaced Phrygia as major power

At height of prosperity under Assyrians, c. 800

Alphabet had developed before 800

Under Assyrian control 671-651

Power broken by Assyrians before 700

Destroyed by Medes and Babylonians in 612

Ravaged by Esarhaddon

Vassal of Esarhaddon

Assyria at accession of Sargon II (c. 720 B.C.)

Assyria at accession of Ashurbanipal (c. 640 B.C.)

MEDIA

ELAM

PERSIAN GULF

Tigris

BABYLONIA

CHALDAEA

URARTU

Lake Van

Nineveh

Euphrates

SYRIA

TAURUS MTS

CILICIA

PHOENICIA

Byblos
Sidon
Tyre

Jerusalem

CYPRUS

Gordium

PHRYGIA

Sardis

LYDIA

EGYPT

Nile

0   200

Miles

11

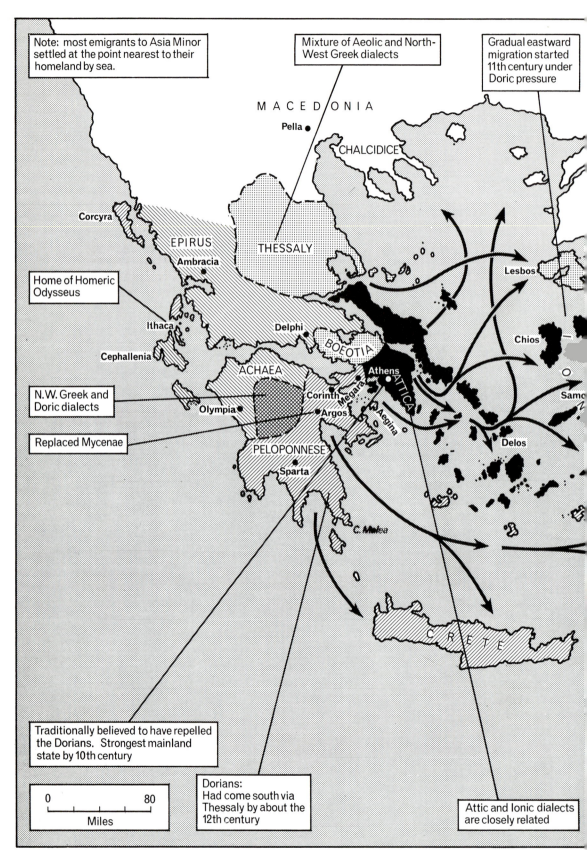

Note: most emigrants to Asia Minor settled at the point nearest to their homeland by sea.

Mixture of Aeolic and North-West Greek dialects

Gradual eastward migration started 11th century under Doric pressure

MACEDONIA

Pella

CHALCIDICE

Corcyra

EPIRUS

Ambracia

THESSALY

Lesbos

Home of Homeric Odysseus

Ithaca

Delphi

Chios

Cephallenia

BOEOTIA

ACHAEA

Athens

N.W. Greek and Doric dialects

Corinth

ATTICA

Megara

Samo

Olympia

Argos

Aegina

Replaced Mycenae

Delos

PELOPONNESE

Sparta

C. Malea

Traditionally believed to have repelled the Dorians. Strongest mainland state by 10th century

CRETE

0   80
Miles

Dorians:
Had come south via Thessaly by about the 12th century

Attic and Ionic dialects are closely related

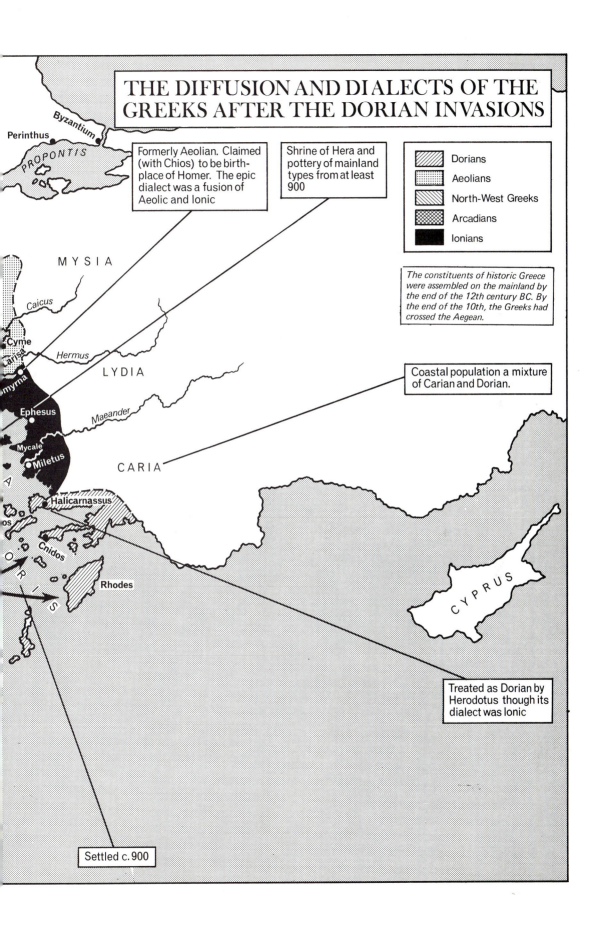

THE DIFFUSION AND DIALECTS OF THE GREEKS AFTER THE DORIAN INVASIONS

Formerly Aeolian. Claimed (with Chios) to be birth-place of Homer. The epic dialect was a fusion of Aeolic and Ionic

Shrine of Hera and pottery of mainland types from at least 900

Dorians
Aeolians
North-West Greeks
Arcadians
Ionians

The constituents of historic Greece were assembled on the mainland by the end of the 12th century BC. By the end of the 10th, the Greeks had crossed the Aegean.

Coastal population a mixture of Carian and Dorian.

Treated as Dorian by Herodotus though its dialect was Ionic

Settled c. 900

PROPONTIS

Perinthus

Byzantium

MYSIA

Caicus

Cyme

Hermus

LYDIA

Smyrna

Ephesus

Maeander

Mycale

Miletus

CARIA

Halicarnassus

Cnidos

Rhodes

CYPRUS

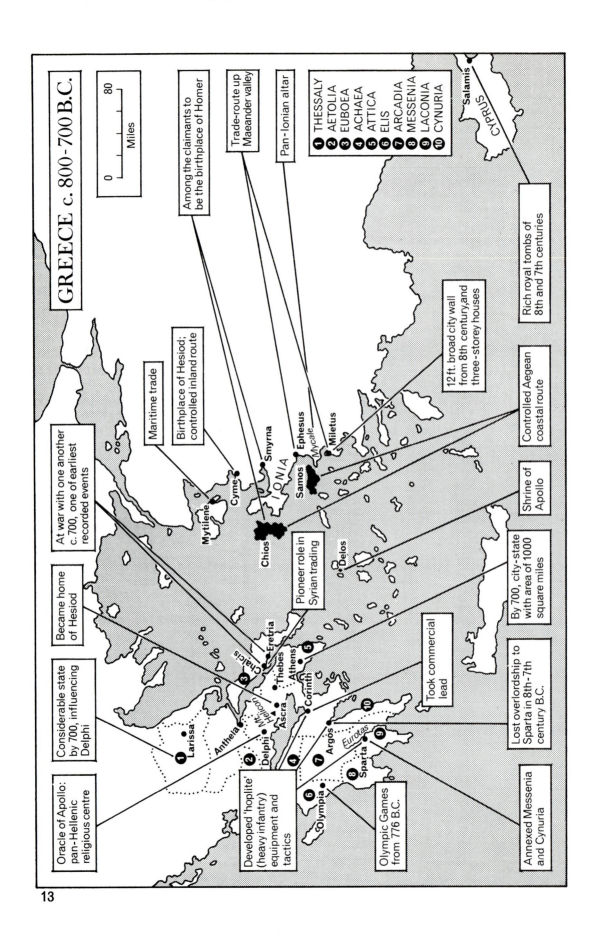

GREECE c. 800–700 B.C.

Miles
0   80

Key
1. THESSALY
2. AETOLIA
3. EUBOEA
4. ACHAEA
5. ATTICA
6. ELIS
7. ARCADIA
8. MESSENIA
9. LACONIA
10. CYNURIA

Among the claimants to be the birthplace of Homer

Trade-route up Maeander valley

Pan-Ionian altar

Maritime trade

Birthplace of Hesiod; controlled inland route

At war with one another c. 700, one of earliest recorded events

Became home of Hesiod

Considerable state by 700, influencing Delphi

Oracle of Apollo: pan-Hellenic religious centre

Developed 'hoplite' (heavy infantry) equipment and tactics

Pioneer role in Syrian trading

12 ft. broad city wall from 8th century, and three-storey houses

Controlled Aegean coastal route

Rich royal tombs of 8th and 7th centuries

Shrine of Apollo

By 700, city-state with area of 1000 square miles

Took commercial lead

Lost overlordship to Sparta in 8th-7th century B.C.

Annexed Messenia and Cynuria

Olympic Games from 776 B.C.

Place labels: Salamis, CYPRUS, Smyrna, Ephesus, Mycale, Miletus, Samos, Cyme, IONIA, Mytilene, Chios, Delos, Eretria, Chalcis, Thebes, Athens, Ascra, Mt. Helicon, Corinth, Larissa, Anthela, Delphi, Argos, Eurotas, Sparta, Olympia

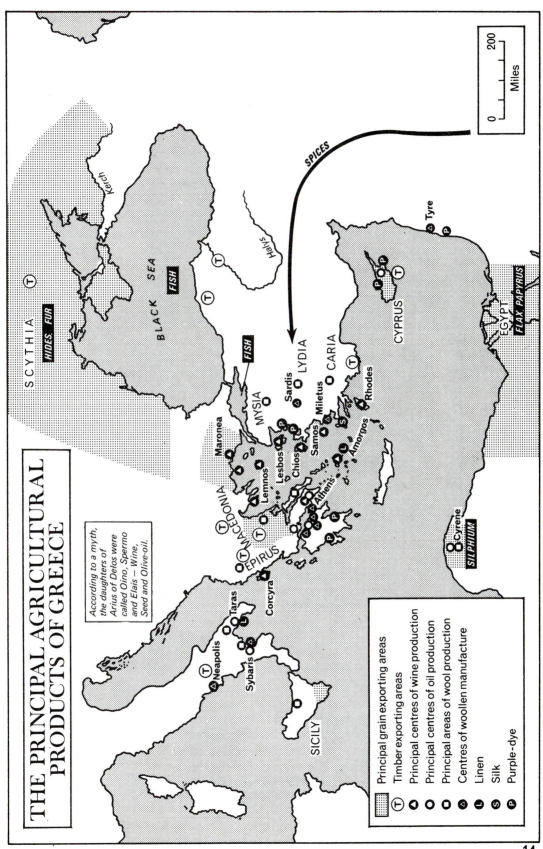

THE PRINCIPAL AGRICULTURAL PRODUCTS OF GREECE

According to a myth,
the daughters of
Arius of Delos were
called Oino, Spermo
and Elais – Wine,
Seed and Olive-oil.

Legend:

Principal grain exporting areas

Ⓣ Timber exporting areas

◓ Principal centres of wine production

Ⓞ Principal centres of oil production

Ⓞ Principal areas of wool production

◭ Centres of woollen manufacture

Ⓛ Linen

Ⓢ Silk

Ⓟ Purple-dye

Labels on map:

SCYTHIA — HIDES, FUR

Kerch

BLACK SEA — FISH

Halys

SPICES

Tyre

CYPRUS

EGYPT — FLAX, PAPYRUS

LYDIA — Sardis

MYSIA

CARIA — Miletus

Rhodes

Amorgos

Samos

Chios

Lesbos

Lemnos

Maronea

MACEDONIA

EPIRUS

Athens

Corcyra

Taras

Neapolis

Sybaris

SICILY

Cyrene — SILPHIUM

FISH

200 Miles

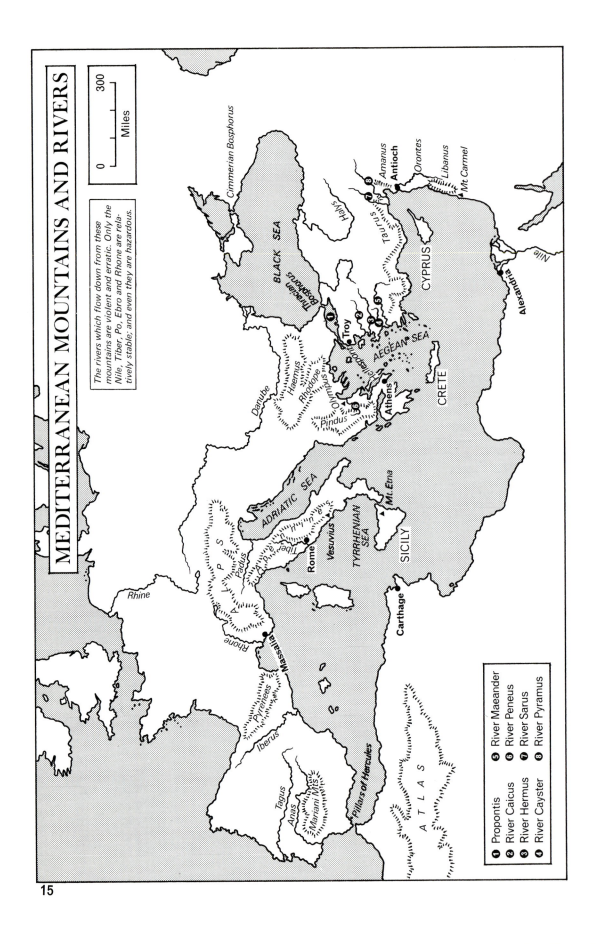

MEDITERRANEAN MOUNTAINS AND RIVERS

The rivers which flow down from these mountains are violent and erratic. Only the Nile, Tiber, Po, Ebro and Rhone are relatively stable; and even they are hazardous.

0   300

Miles

Cimmerian Bosphorus

BLACK SEA

Thracian Bosphorus

Halys

Amanus
Antioch
Orontes
Libanus
Mt. Carmel

Taurus

CYPRUS

Nile

Alexandria

AEGEAN SEA

Troy

Chalcidice

Danube

Haemus

Rhodope

Olympus

Pindus

Athens

CRETE

ADRIATIC SEA

A P e n n i n e s

Padus

A L P S

Tiber

Vesuvius

Rome

Mt. Etna

TYRRHENIAN SEA

SICILY

Carthage

Rhine

Rhone

Pyrenees

Massalia

Iberus

Tagus

Anas

Mariani Mts

Pillars of Hercules

A T L A S

❶ Propontis	❺ River Maeander	
❷ River Caicus	❻ River Peneus	
❸ River Hermus	❼ River Sarus	
❹ River Cayster	❽ River Pyramus	

15

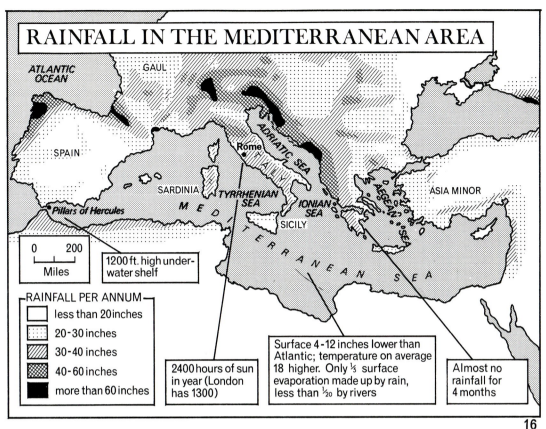

RAINFALL IN THE MEDITERRANEAN AREA

ATLANTIC OCEAN

GAUL

SPAIN

Pillars of Hercules

SARDINIA

Rome

ADRIATIC SEA

TYRRHENIAN SEA

IONIAN SEA

SICILY

MEDITERRANEAN SEA

AEGEAN SEA

ASIA MINOR

0   200
Miles

1200 ft. high under-water shelf

RAINFALL PER ANNUM

less than 20 inches

20-30 inches

30-40 inches

40-60 inches

more than 60 inches

2400 hours of sun in year (London has 1300)

Surface 4-12 inches lower than Atlantic; temperature on average 18 higher. Only ⅕ surface evaporation made up by rain, less than ¹⁄₂₀ by rivers

Almost no rainfall for 4 months

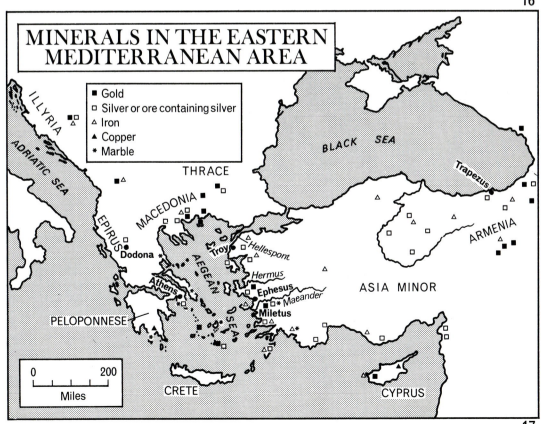

MINERALS IN THE EASTERN MEDITERRANEAN AREA

■ Gold
□ Silver or ore containing silver
△ Iron
▲ Copper
✳ Marble

ILLYRIA

ADRIATIC SEA

EPIRUS

THRACE

MACEDONIA

BLACK SEA

Trapezus

Dodona

Troy

Hellespont

Hermus

AEGEAN SEA

Ephesus

Maeander

Miletus

ASIA MINOR

ARMENIA

Athens

PELOPONNESE

CRETE

CYPRUS

0   200
Miles

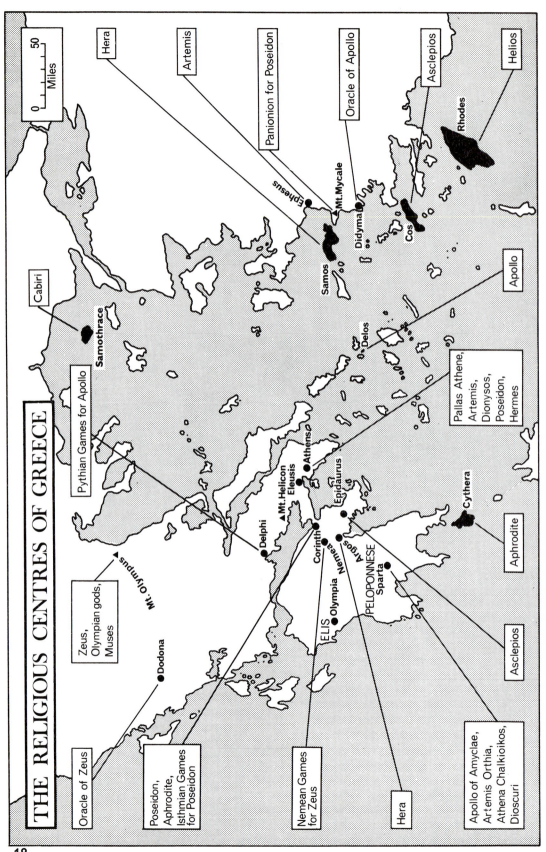

THE RELIGIOUS CENTRES OF GREECE

Oracle of Zeus

Zeus, Olympian gods, Muses

Pythian Games for Apollo

Poseidon, Aphrodite, Isthmian Games for Poseidon

Hera

Cabiri

Samothrace

Nemean Games for Zeus

Apollo of Amyclae, Artemis Orthia, Athena Chalkioikos, Dioscuri

Asclepios

Aphrodite

Apollo

Pallas Athene, Artemis, Dionysos, Poseidon, Hermes

Hera

Artemis

Panionion for Poseidon

Oracle of Apollo

Asclepios

Helios

Mt.Olympus

Dodona

Delphi

Mt.Helicon
Eleusis

Athens

Epidaurus

Corinth
Nemea
Argos

ELIS
Olympia

PELOPONNESE
Sparta

Cythera

Ephesus

Mt.Mycale

Didyma

Cos

Samos

Delos

Rhodes

Miles
0   50

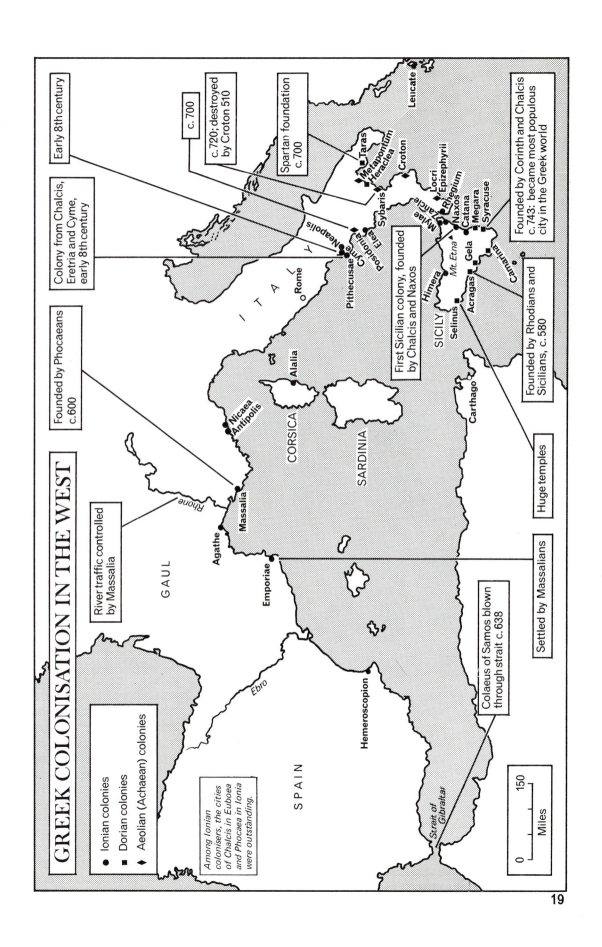

GREEK COLONISATION IN THE WEST

Ionian colonies ●
Dorian colonies ■
Aeolian (Achaean) colonies ◆

Among Ionian colonisers, the cities of Chalcis in Euboea and Phocaea in Ionia were outstanding.

Early 8th century

c. 700

c.720; destroyed by Croton 510

Spartan foundation c.700

Colony from Chalcis, Eretria and Cyme, early 8th century

Founded by Corinth and Chalcis c.743: became most populous city in the Greek world

First Sicilian colony, founded by Chalcis and Naxos

Founded by Rhodians and Sicilians, c.580

Huge temples

Founded by Phocaeans c.600

River traffic controlled by Massalia

Settled by Massalians

Colaeus of Samos blown through strait c.638

Leucate

Taras
Metapontum
Heraclea
Croton
Locri
Epizephyrii
Rhegium
Naxos
Catana
Megara
Syracuse
Sybaris
Mylae
Zancle
Himera
Mt. Etna
Gela
Selinus
Acragas
Camarina

SICILY

Neapolis
Cyme
Pithecusae
Posidonia
Elea
Rome

I T A L Y

Alalia
Nicaea
Antipolis
CORSICA
SARDINIA
Massalia
Agathe
Emporiae
Carthago

Rhone
GAUL

S P A I N
Ebro
Hemeroscopion

Strait of Gibraltar

0   150
Miles

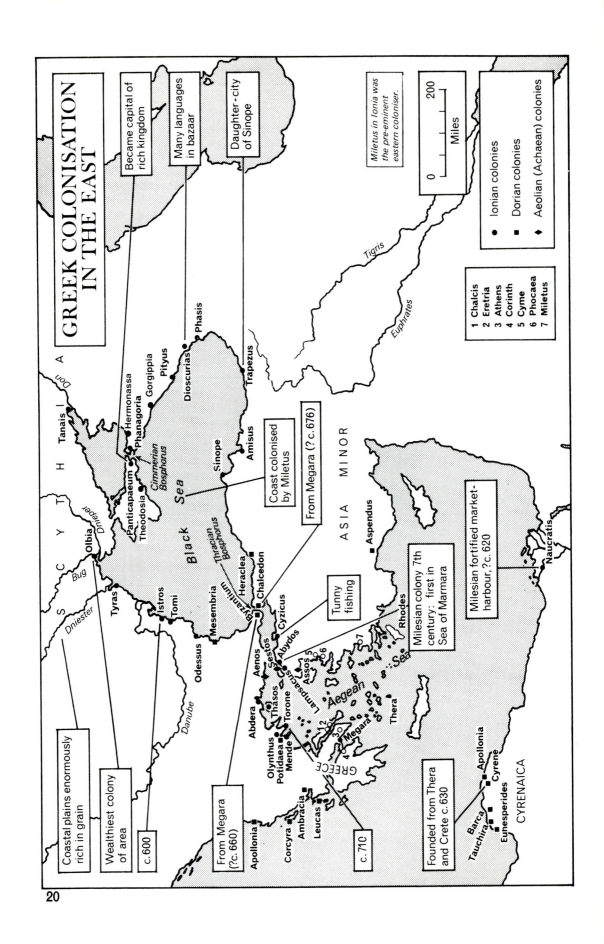

GREEK COLONISATION IN THE EAST

Became capital of rich kingdom

Many languages in bazaar

Daughter-city of Sinope

Miletus in Ionia was the pre-eminent eastern coloniser.

0   200
Miles

● Ionian colonies
■ Dorian colonies
◆ Aeolian (Achaean) colonies

1 Chalcis
2 Eretria
3 Athens
4 Corinth
5 Cyme
6 Phocaea
7 Miletus

Tigris

Euphrates

S C Y T H I A

Don

Tanais

Hermonassa
Phanagoria
Gorgippia
Pityus
Phasis

Panticapaeum
Theodosia
Cimmerian Bosphorus

Dioscurias

Trapezus

Amisus

Sinope

Coast colonised by Miletus

From Megara (? c. 676)

Black Sea

A S I A   M I N O R

Olbia
Dnieper

Bug

Tyras
Dniester

Istros
Tomi

Danube

Odessus

Mesembria

Thracian Bosphorus
Heraclea
Byzantium
Chalcedon
Cyzicus

Aspendus

Tunny fishing

Milesian colony 7th century: first in Sea of Marmara

Milesian fortified market-harbour, ? c. 620

Rhodes

Aenos
Sestos
Abydos
Lampsacus
Assos 5
6
7

Aegean Sea

Abdera
Thasos
Torone

Thera

Coastal plains enormously rich in grain

Wealthiest colony of area

c. 600

From Megara (? c. 660)

Olynthus
Potidaea
Mende

Megara

GREECE

Apollonia

Corcyra
Ambracia
Leucas

c. 710

Founded from Thera and Crete c. 630

Naucratis

Apollonia
Cyrene
Barca
Tauchira
Euesperides

CYRENAICA

20

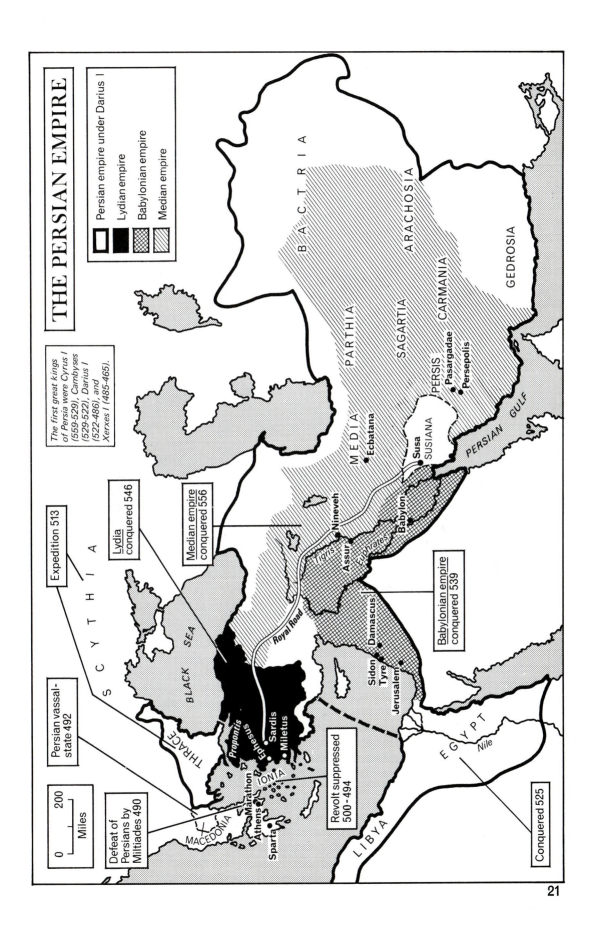

THE PERSIAN EMPIRE

Persian empire under Darius I

Lydian empire

Babylonian empire

Median empire

The first great kings of Persia were Cyrus I (559-529), Cambyses (529-522), Darius I (522-486), and Xerxes I (485-465).

Expedition 513

Lydia conquered 546

Median empire conquered 556

Babylonian empire conquered 539

Persian vassal-state 492

Defeat of Persians by Miltiades 490

Revolt suppressed 500-494

Conquered 525

0 200

Miles

SCYTHIA

THRACE

BLACK SEA

MACEDONIA

Marathon

Athens

Sparta

IONIA

Propontis

Ephesus

Sardis

Miletus

Royal Road

LIBYA

EGYPT

Nile

Sidon

Tyre

Jerusalem

Damascus

Assur

Nineveh

Tigris

Euphrates

Babylon

Susa

SUSIANA

Ecbatana

MEDIA

PARTHIA

BACTRIA

SAGARTIA

ARACHOSIA

PERSIS

Pasargadae

Persepolis

CARMANIA

GEDROSIA

PERSIAN GULF

21

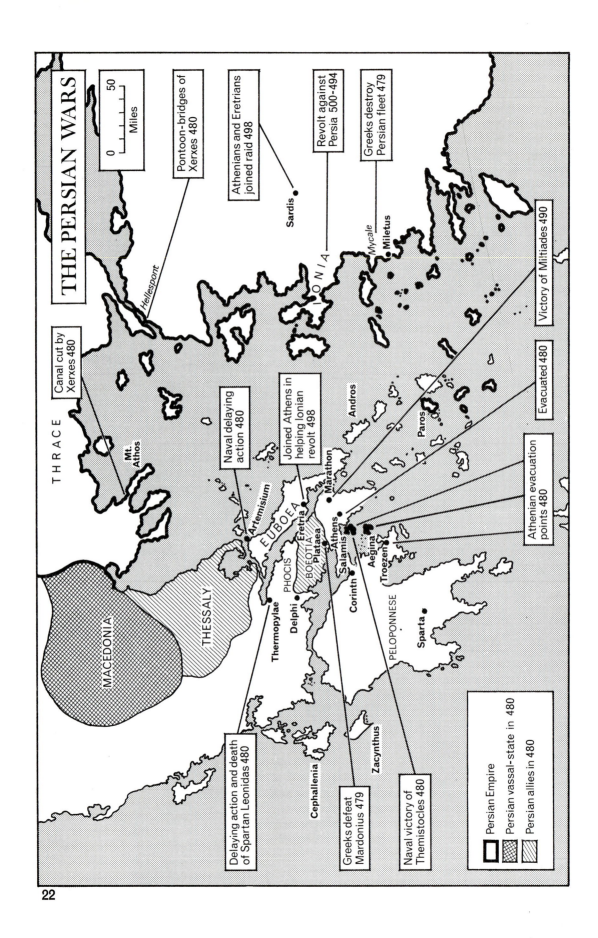

THE PERSIAN WARS

Miles

0   50

Pontoon-bridges of Xerxes 480

Athenians and Eretrians joined raid 498

Revolt against Persia 500-494

Greeks destroy Persian fleet 479

Canal cut by Xerxes 480

Naval delaying action 480

Joined Athens in helping Ionian revolt 498

Victory of Miltiades 490

Evacuated 480

Athenian evacuation points 480

Delaying action and death of Spartan Leonidas 480

Greeks defeat Mardonius 479

Naval victory of Themistocles 480

THRACE

MACEDONIA

THESSALY

PHOCIS

BOEOTIA

EUBOEA

Mt. Athos

Hellespont

Sardis

Mycale

Miletus

IONIA

Andros

Paros

Artemisium

Eretria

Marathon

Plataea

Athens

Salamis

Aegina

Corinth

Troezen

Delphi

Thermopylae

Cephallenia

Zacynthus

Sparta

PELOPONNESE

Persian Empire

Persian vassal-state in 480

Persian allies in 480

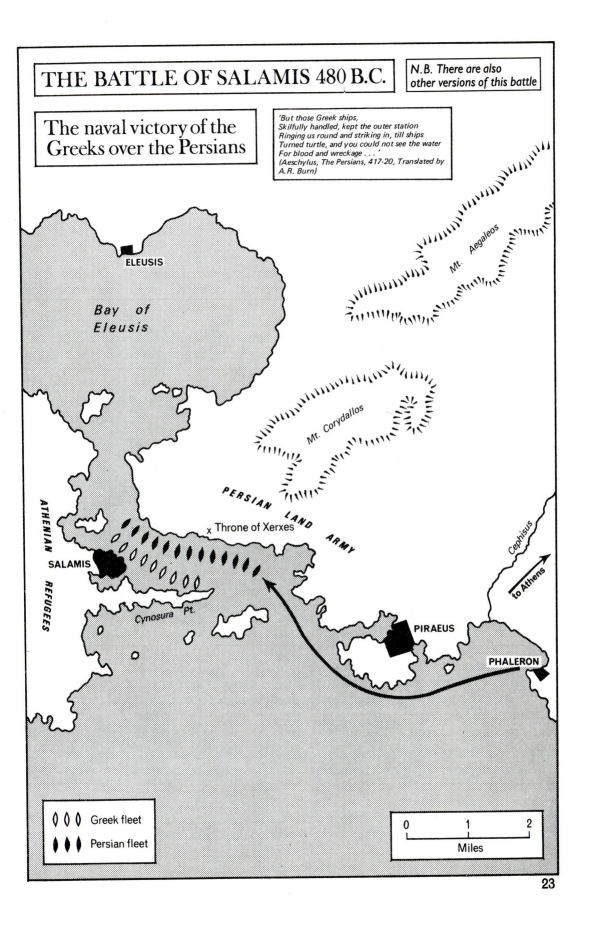

THE BATTLE OF SALAMIS 480 B.C.

N.B. There are also other versions of this battle

The naval victory of the Greeks over the Persians

'But those Greek ships,
Skilfully handled, kept the outer station
Ringing us round and striking in, till ships
Turned turtle, and you could not see the water
For blood and wreckage . . .'
(Aeschylus, The Persians, 417-20, Translated by A.R. Burn)

ELEUSIS

Bay of Eleusis

Mt. Aegaleos

Mt. Corydallos

PERSIAN LAND ARMY

x Throne of Xerxes

Cephisus

to Athens

ATHENIAN REFUGEES

SALAMIS

Cynosura Pt.

PIRAEUS

PHALERON

◊ ◊ ◊ Greek fleet

◆ ◆ ◆ Persian fleet

0   1   2
Miles

23

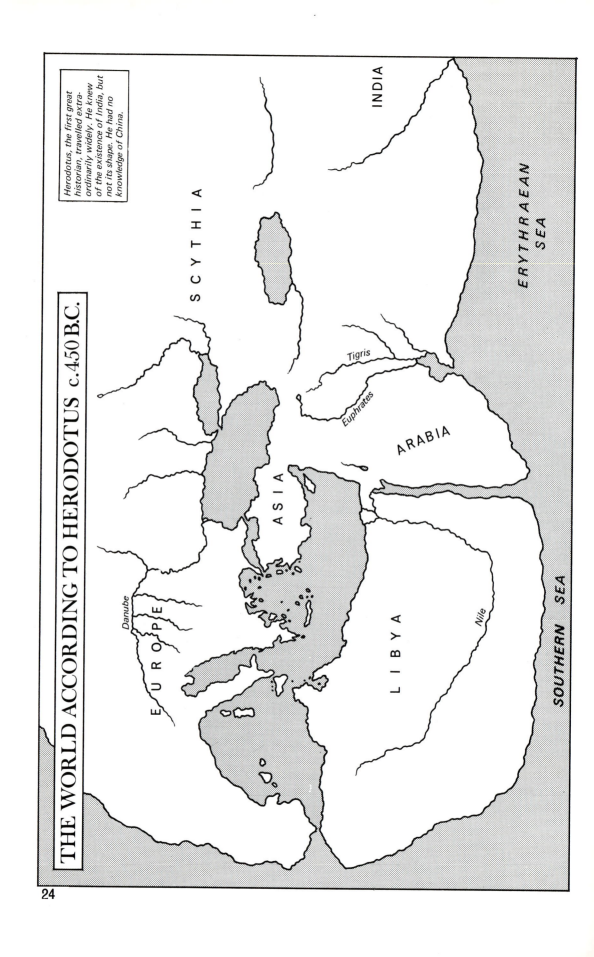

THE WORLD ACCORDING TO HERODOTUS c.450 B.C.

Herodotus, the first great historian, travelled extraordinarily widely. He knew of the existence of India, but not its shape. He had no knowledge of China.

INDIA

ERYTHRAEAN SEA

SCYTHIA

Tigris

Euphrates

ARABIA

ASIA

Danube

EUROPE

LIBYA

Nile

SOUTHERN SEA

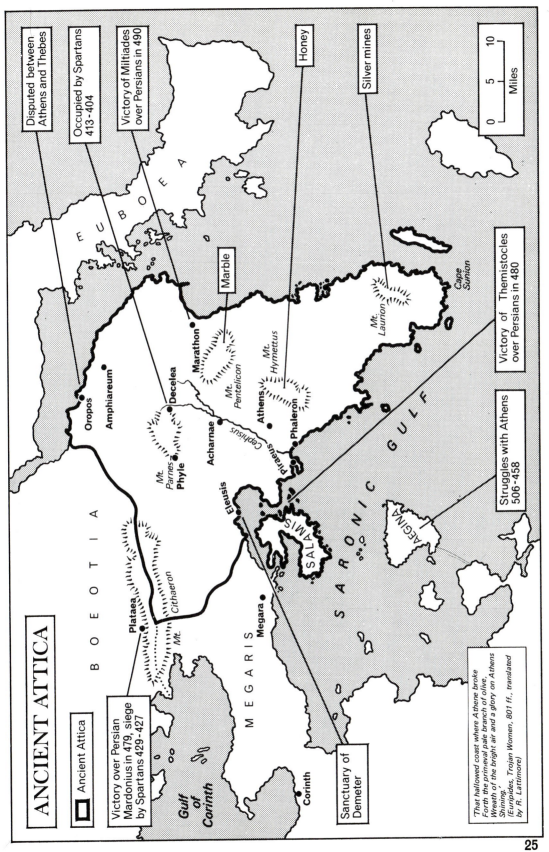

ANCIENT ATTICA

□ Ancient Attica

Victory over Persian Mardonius in 479, siege by Spartans 429-427

Disputed between Athens and Thebes

Occupied by Spartans 413-404

Victory of Miltiades over Persians in 490

Honey

Silver mines

Marble

Victory of Themistocles over Persians in 480

Struggles with Athens 506-458

Sanctuary of Demeter

EUBOEA

BOEOTIA

MEGARIS

Gulf of Corinth

Corinth

Megara

Plataea

Mt. Cithaeron

Eleusis

SALAMIS

Mt. Parnes

Phyle

Acharnae

Cephisus

Piraeus

Athens

Phaleron

Mt. Pentelicon

Mt. Hymettus

Decelea

Marathon

Oropos

Amphiareum

Mt. Laurion

Cape Sunian

SARONIC GULF

AEGINA

'That hallowed coast where Athene broke
Forth the primeval pale branch of olive,
Wreath of the bright air and a glory on Athens
Shining.'
(Euripides, Trojan Women, 801 ff., translated
by R. Lattimore)

0   5   10
Miles

25

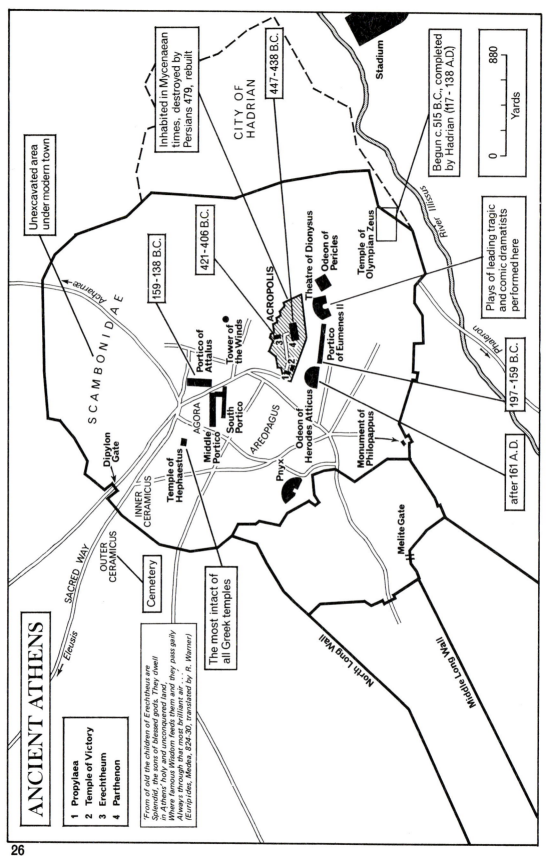

ANCIENT ATHENS

1 Propylaea
2 Temple of Victory
3 Erechtheum
4 Parthenon

'From of old the children of Erechtheus are
Splendid, the sons of blessed gods. They dwell
in Athens' holy and unconquered land,
Where famous Wisdom feeds them and they pass gaily
Always through that most brilliant air . . .'
(Euripides, Medea, 824-30, translated by R. Warner)

Cemetery

The most intact of
all Greek temples

Unexcavated area
under modern town

Inhabited in Mycenaean
times, destroyed by
Persians 479, rebuilt

159 - 138 B.C.

421 - 406 B.C.

447 - 438 B.C.

CITY OF
HADRIAN

Begun c. 515 B.C., completed
by Hadrian (117 - 138 A.D.)

0   880
Yards

Plays of leading tragic
and comic dramatists
performed here

197 - 159 B.C.

after 161 A.D.

Stadium

River Illisus

Phaleron

Temple of
Olympian Zeus

Odeon of
Pericles

Theatre of Dionysus

ACROPOLIS

Portico
of Eumenes II

Portico of Attalus

Tower of
the Winds

Odeon of
Herodes Atticus

Monument of
Philopappus

AGORA

South Portico

Middle
Portico

AREOPAGUS

Pnyx

Temple of
Hephaestus

INNER
CERAMICUS

OUTER
CERAMICUS

Dipylon
Gate

S C A M B O N I D A E

Acharnae

SACRED WAY

Eleusis

Melite Gate

North Long Wall

Middle Long Wall

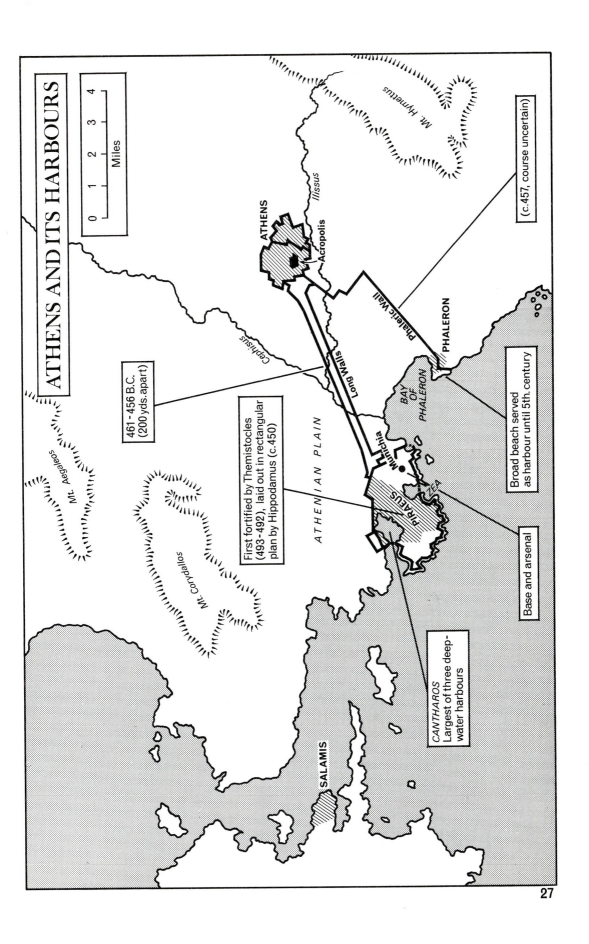

ATHENS AND ITS HARBOURS

Miles
0 1 2 3 4

Mt. Aegaleos

Mt. Corydallos

ATHENIAN PLAIN

Cephisus

Ilissus

ATHENS
Acropolis

Mt. Hymettus

461 - 456 B.C.
(200 yds. apart)

Long Walls

Phaleric Wall

PHALERON

BAY OF PHALERON

(c.457, course uncertain)

Broad beach served
as harbour until 5th. century

First fortified by Themistocles
(493 - 492), laid out in rectangular
plan by Hippodamus (c.450)

Munichia

PIRAEUS

Base and arsenal

CANTHAROS
Largest of three deep-
water harbours

SALAMIS

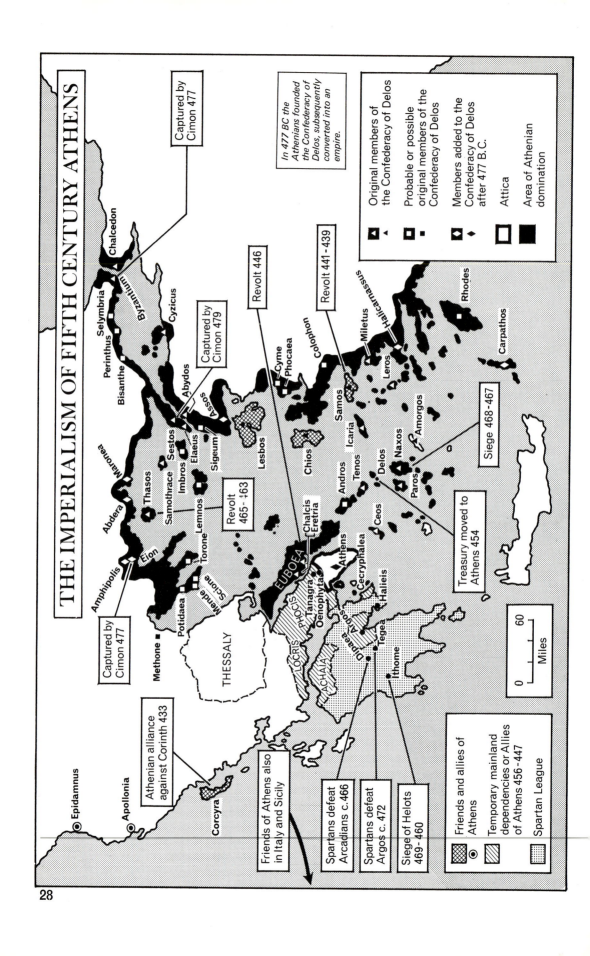

THE IMPERIALISM OF FIFTH CENTURY ATHENS

In 477 BC the Athenians founded the Confederacy of Delos, subsequently converted into an empire.

Original members of the Confederacy of Delos

Probable or possible original members of the Confederacy of Delos

Members added to the Confederacy of Delos after 477 B.C.

Attica

Area of Athenian domination

Captured by Cimon 477

Captured by Cimon 479

Revolt 446

Revolt 441 - 439

Revolt 465 - 463

Treasury moved to Athens 454

Siege 468 - 467

Captured by Cimon 477

Athenian alliance against Corinth 433

Friends of Athens also in Italy and Sicily

Spartans defeat Arcadians c.466

Spartans defeat Argos c. 472

Siege of Helots 469 - 460

Friends and allies of Athens

Temporary mainland dependencies or Allies of Athens 456 - 447

Spartan League

Chalcedon

Byzantium

Selymbria
Perinthus
Bisanthe
Cyzicus

Maroneca

Abdera

Thasos

Samothrace
Imbros
Abydos
Assos
Sestos
Elaeus
Sigeum
Lemnos
Amphipolis
Eion
Torone
Methone
Potidaea
Mende
Scione

Cyme
Phocaea
Colophon

Miletus
Halicarnassus

Rhodes

Carpathos

Lesbos

Chios

Samos
Icaria
Leros

Andros
Tenos
Delos
Naxos
Paros
Amorgos

Ceos

Chalcis
Eretria
EUBOEA

Athens
Cecryphalea
Haliels

LOCRIS
PHOCIS
Tanagra
Oenophyta
Plataea
Aegina
Tegea
Ithome
ACHAIA

THESSALY

Epidamnus

Apollonia

Corcyra

0   60
Miles

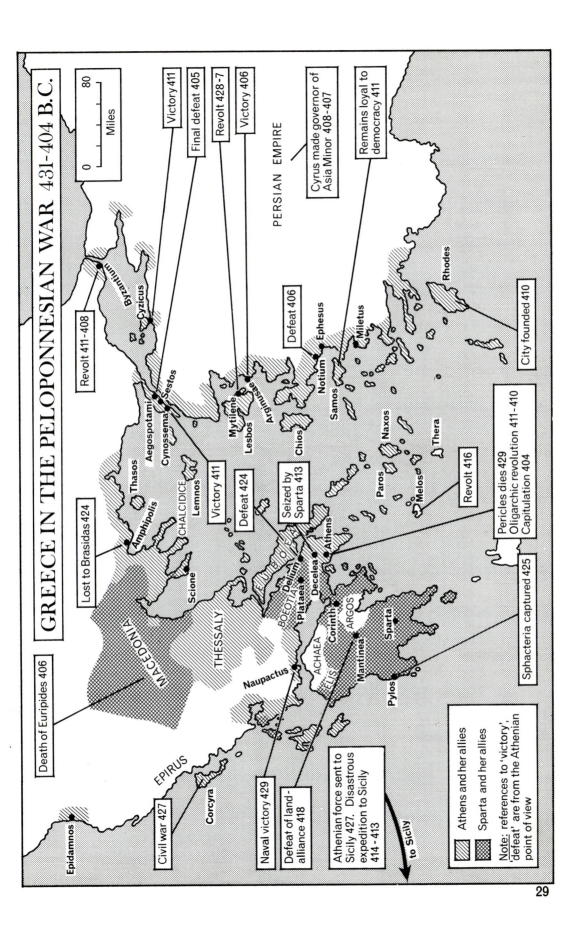

GREECE IN THE PELOPONNESIAN WAR 431-404 B.C.

Miles
0   80

Death of Euripides 406

Civil war 427

EPIRUS

Corcyra

Epidamnos

MACEDONIA

Amphipolis

Lost to Brasidas 424

Scione

CHALCIDICE

Thasos

Byzantium

Revolt 411-408

Aegospotami
Sestos
Cynossema

Victory 411

Final defeat 405

Revolt 428-7

Victory 406

Cyrus made governor of
Asia Minor 408-407

Remains loyal to
democracy 411

PERSIAN EMPIRE

Cyzicus

Lemnos

Victory 411

Defeat 424

Mytilene
Lesbos

Arginusae

Chios

Notium
Ephesus

Defeat 406

Samos

Miletus

Rhodes

THESSALY

Naupactus

ACHAEA
ELIS

Mantinea

Pylos

Sphacteria captured 425

Naval victory 429

Defeat of land-
alliance 418

Athenian force sent to
Sicily 427. Disastrous
expedition to Sicily
414 - 413

to Sicily

Seized by
Sparta 413

BOEOTIA
Delium
Plataea
Decelea
EUBOEA
Athens
Corinth
ARGOS
Sparta

Naxos
Paros
Melos
Thera

Revolt 416

Pericles dies 429
Oligarchic revolution 411-410
Capitulation 404

City founded 410

Athens and her allies

Sparta and her allies

Note: references to 'victory',
'defeat' are from the Athenian
point of view

29

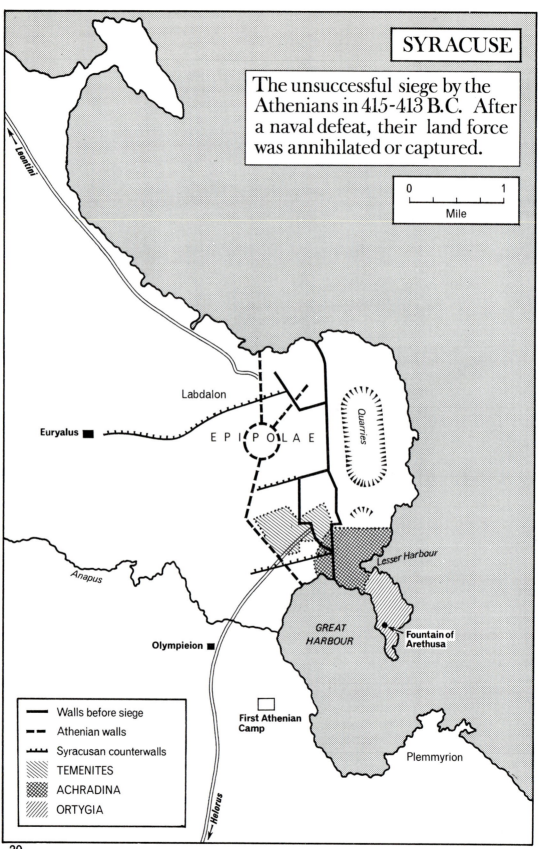

SYRACUSE

The unsuccessful siege by the Athenians in 415-413 B.C. After a naval defeat, their land force was annihilated or captured.

0   1
Mile

Leontini

Labdalon

Euryalus ■

E P I P O L A E

Quarries

Anapus

Lesser Harbour

Olympieion ■

GREAT
HARBOUR

Fountain of
Arethusa

First Athenian
Camp

Plemmyrion

——— Walls before siege
- - - Athenian walls
++++ Syracusan counterwalls
▨ TEMENITES
▨ ACHRADINA
▨ ORTYGIA

Helorus

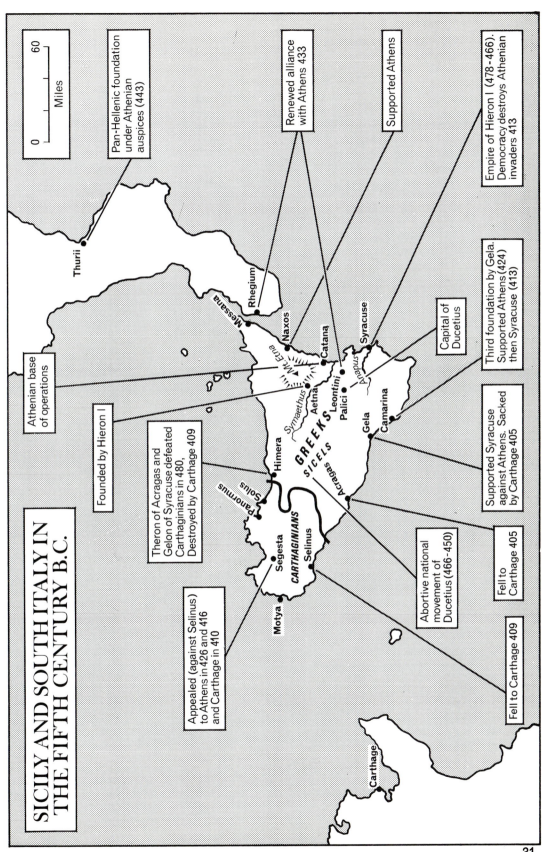

SICILY AND SOUTH ITALY IN THE FIFTH CENTURY B.C.

0 _____ 60

Miles

Pan-Hellenic foundation under Athenian auspices (443)

Renewed alliance with Athens 433

Supported Athens

Empire of Hieron I (478–466). Democracy destroys Athenian invaders 413

Athenian base of operations

Founded by Hieron I

Theron of Acragas and Gelon of Syracuse defeated Carthaginians in 480, Destroyed by Carthage 409

Appealed (against Selinus) to Athens in 426 and 416 and Carthage in 410

Capital of Ducetius

Third foundation by Gela. Supported Athens (424) then Syracuse (413)

Supported Syracuse against Athens. Sacked by Carthage 405

Abortive national movement of Ducetius (466–450)

Fell to Carthage 405

Fell to Carthage 409

Thurii

Rhegium

Messana

Naxos

Catana

Syracuse

Mt Etna

Symaethus

Aetna

Leontini

Palici

Anapus

GREEKS

SICELS

Gela

Camarina

Himera

Panormus

Solus

CARTHAGINIANS

Segesta

Selinus

Acragas

Motya

Carthage

31

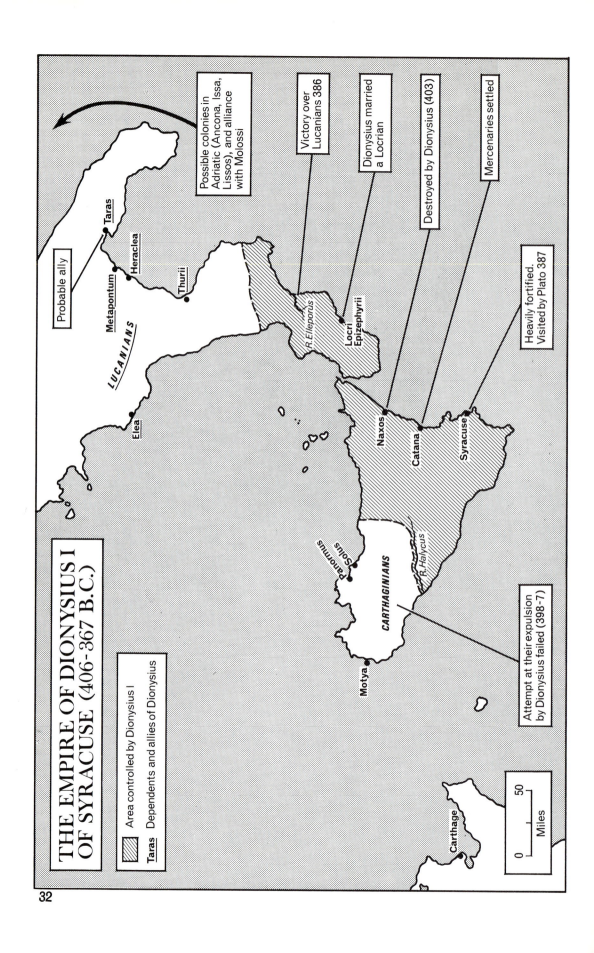

THE EMPIRE OF DIONYSIUS I OF SYRACUSE (406–367 B.C.)

▨ Area controlled by Dionysius I

<u>Taras</u> Dependents and allies of Dionysius

Possible colonies in Adriatic (Ancona, Issa, Lissos), and alliance with Molossi

Probable ally

Taras
Heraclea
Metapontum
Thurii

LUCANIANS

Elea

Victory over Lucanians 386

Dionysius married a Locrian

Destroyed by Dionysius (403)

Mercenaries settled

Heavily fortified. Visited by Plato 387

R. Eleporus

Locri Epizephyrii

Naxos
Catana
Syracuse

Solus
Panormus

CARTHAGINIANS

R. Halycus

Attempt at their expulsion by Dionysius failed (398–7)

Motya

Carthage

50

Miles

0

32

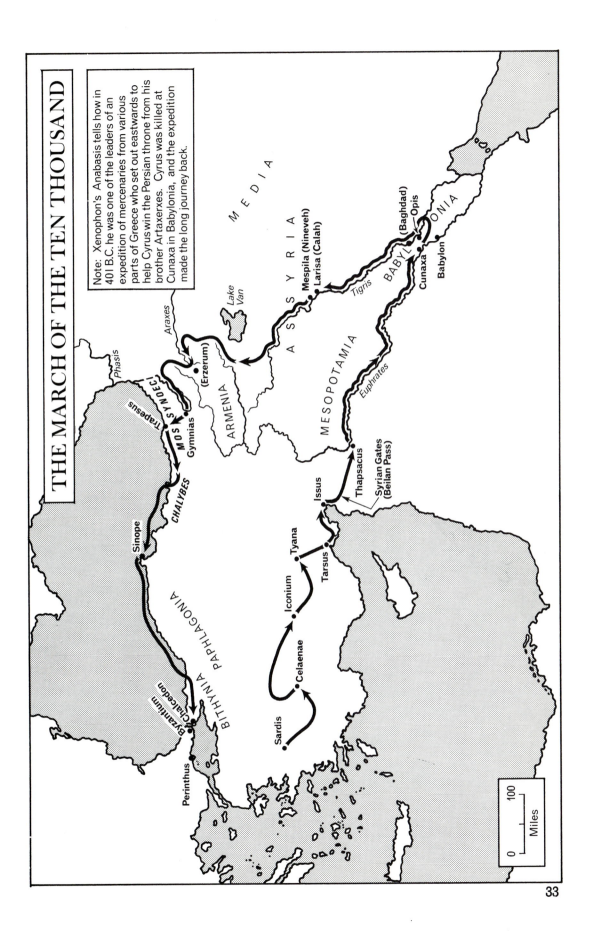

THE MARCH OF THE TEN THOUSAND

Note: Xenophon's Anabasis tells how in 401 B.C. he was one of the leaders of an expedition of mercenaries from various parts of Greece who set out eastwards to help Cyrus win the Persian throne from his brother Artaxerxes. Cyrus was killed at Cunaxa in Babylonia, and the expedition made the long journey back.

MEDIA

ASSYRIA

Mespila (Nineveh)
Larisa (Calah)

Tigris

BABYL...ONIA

Opis
(Baghdad)

Cunaxa

Babylon

Lake Van

Araxes

Phasis

(Erzerum)

ARMENIA

MESOPOTAMIA

Euphrates

M O S · S Y N O E C I

Trapesus

Gymnias

CHALYBES

Thapsacus

Syrian Gates
(Beilan Pass)

Issus

Sinope

Tyana

Iconium

Tarsus

PAPHLAGONIA

BITHYNIA

Celaenae

Byzantium

Chalcedon

Perinthus

Sardis

| 0 | 100 |
Miles

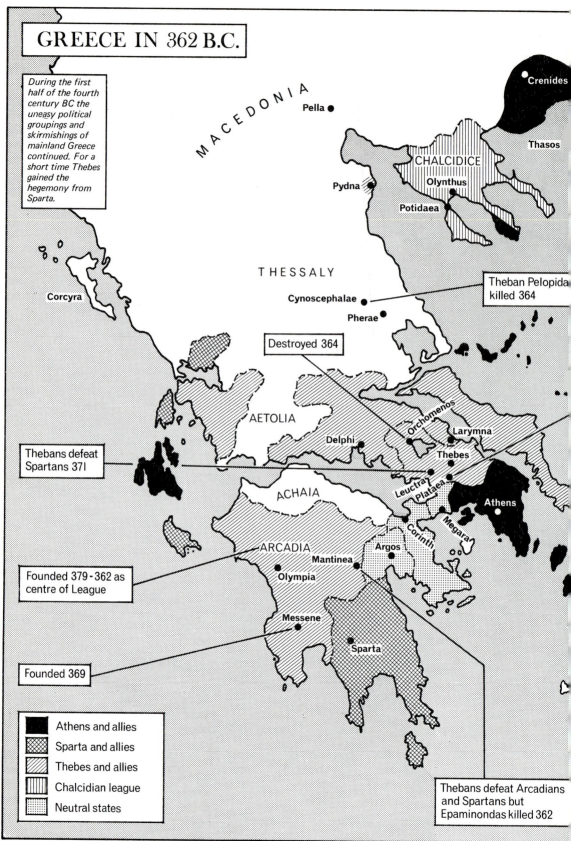

GREECE IN 362 B.C.

During the first half of the fourth century BC the uneasy political groupings and skirmishings of mainland Greece continued. For a short time Thebes gained the hegemony from Sparta.

MACEDONIA

Crenides

Pella

Thasos

CHALCIDICE

Olynthus

Pydna

Potidaea

THESSALY

Theban Pelopidas killed 364

Cynoscephalae

Corcyra

Pherae

Destroyed 364

AETOLIA

Orchomenos

Larymna

Delphi

Thebes

Thebans defeat Spartans 371

Leuctra

Plataea

ACHAIA

Athens

Corinth

Megara

ARCADIA

Argos

Founded 379 - 362 as centre of League

Mantinea

Olympia

Messene

Sparta

Founded 369

■	Athens and allies
▨	Sparta and allies
▨	Thebes and allies
▥	Chalcidian league
▨	Neutral states

Thebans defeat Arcadians and Spartans but Epaminondas killed 362

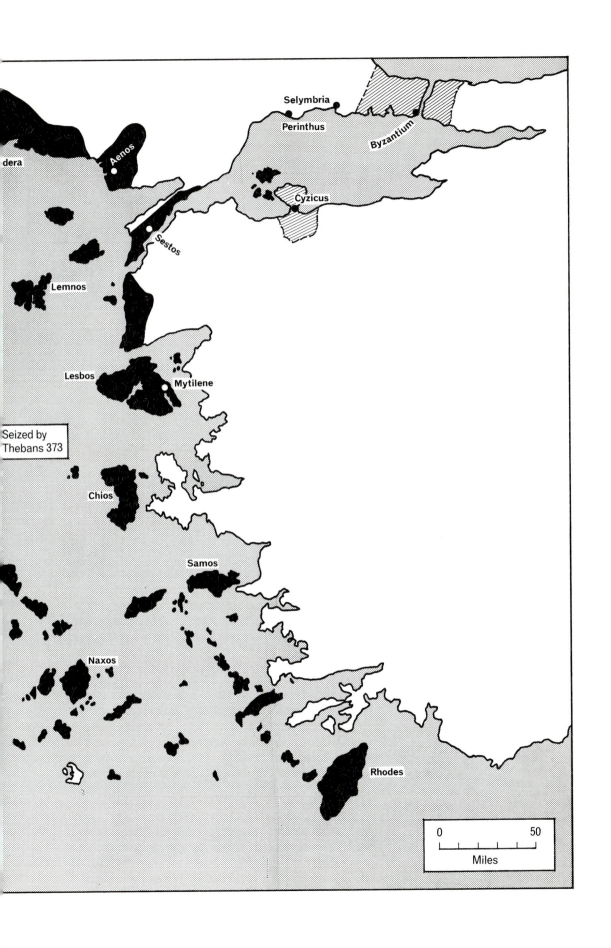

Selymbria

Perinthus

Byzantium

dera

Aenos

Cyzicus

Sestos

Lemnos

Lesbos

Mytilene

Seized by
Thebans 373

Chios

Samos

Naxos

Rhodes

0   50
Miles

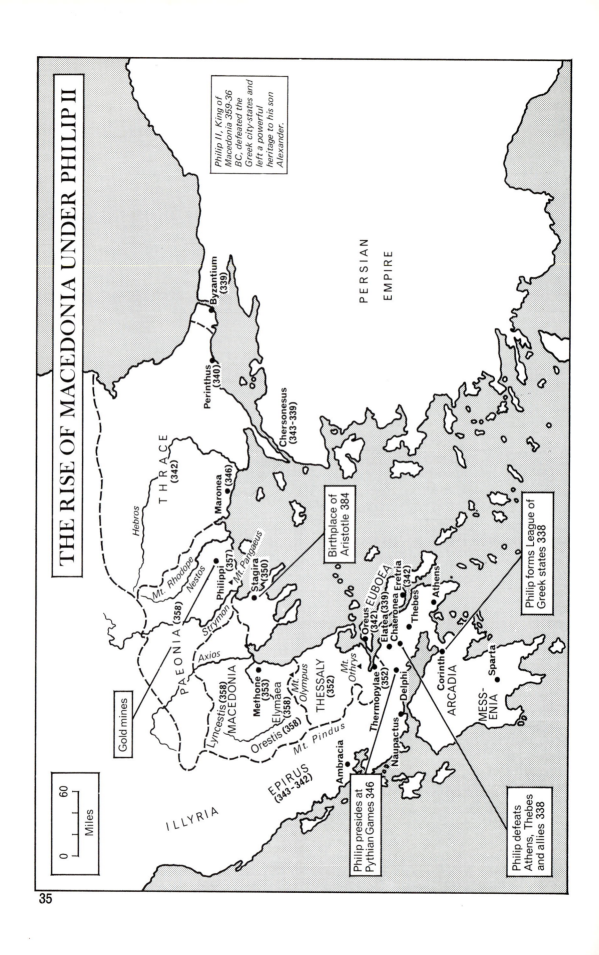

THE RISE OF MACEDONIA UNDER PHILIP II

Philip II, King of Macedonia 359-36 BC, defeated the Greek city-states and left a powerful heritage to his son Alexander.

PERSIAN EMPIRE

Byzantium (339)

Perinthus (340)

Chersonesus (343-339)

THRACE (342)

Hebros

Maronea (346)

Mt. Rhodope

Nestos

Philippi (357)

Mt. Pangaeus

Stagira (350)

Birthplace of Aristotle 384

Strymon

PAEONIA (358)

Axios

EUBOEA

Oreus (342)

Elatea (339)

Chaeronea Eretria (342)

Thebes

Athens

Lyncestis (358)

MACEDONIA

Methone (353)

Elymaea (358)

Orestis (358)

Mt. Olympus

THESSALY (352)

Mt. Othrys

Mt. Pindus

Thermopylae (352)

Naupactus

Delphi

Corinth

ARCADIA

MESS-ENIA

Sparta

Philip forms League of Greek states 338

Gold mines

EPIRUS (343-342)

Ambracia

ILLYRIA

Philip presides at Pythian Games 346

Philip defeats Athens, Thebes and allies 338

Miles

0   60

35

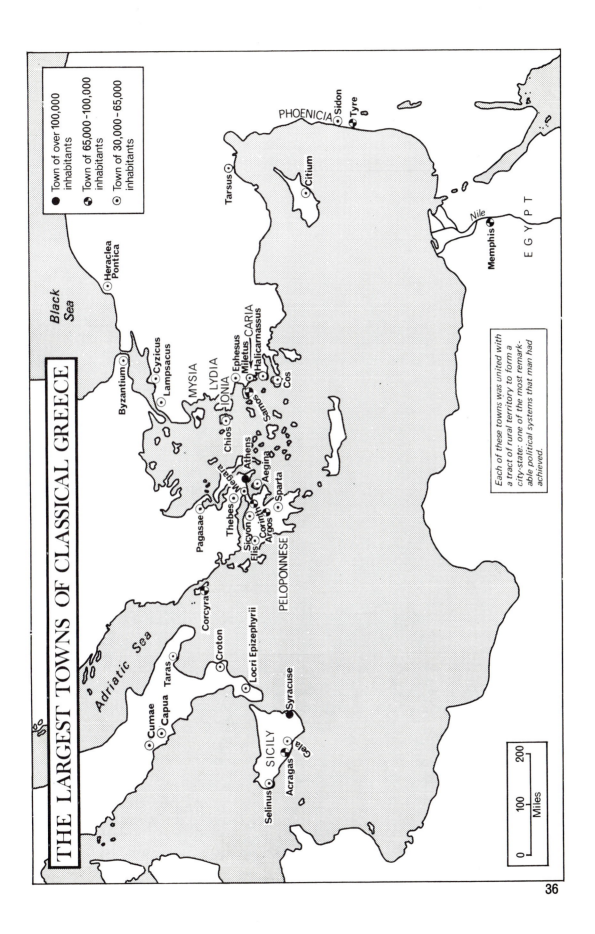

THE LARGEST TOWNS OF CLASSICAL GREECE

Legend:
- Town of over 100,000 inhabitants
- Town of 65,000 – 100,000 inhabitants
- Town of 30,000 – 65,000 inhabitants

Each of these towns was united with a tract of rural territory to form a city-state: one of the most remarkable political systems that man had achieved.

Black Sea

Adriatic Sea

PHOENICIA
Sidon
Tyre

Citium

Tarsus

Nile
Memphis

E G Y P T

Heraclea Pontica

Cyzicus
Lampsacus

Byzantium

MYSIA
LYDIA
IONIA
Ephesus
Miletus CARIA
Halicarnassus
Cos

Chios
Samos

Pagasae

Thebes
Megara
Athens
Sicyon
Elis
Corinth
Aegina
Argos
Sparta

PELOPONNESE

Corcyra

Croton

Locri Epizephyrii

Taras

Cumae
Capua

Syracuse

Gela

SICILY
Selinus
Acragas

0   100   200
Miles

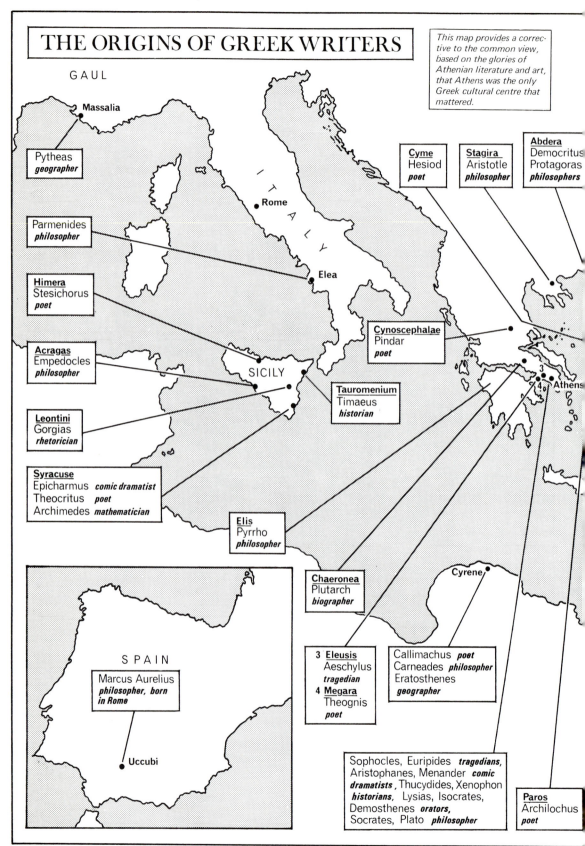

THE ORIGINS OF GREEK WRITERS

This map provides a corrective to the common view, based on the glories of Athenian literature and art, that Athens was the only Greek cultural centre that mattered.

GAUL

Massalia

Pytheas
geographer

Parmenides
philosopher

Himera
Stesichorus
poet

Acragas
Empedocles
philosopher

Leontini
Gorgias
rhetorician

Syracuse
Epicharmus *comic dramatist*
Theocritus *poet*
Archimedes *mathematician*

Elis
Pyrrho
philosopher

ITALY

Rome

Elea

SICILY

Cynoscephalae
Pindar
poet

Tauromenium
Timaeus
historian

Cyme
Hesiod
poet

Stagira
Aristotle
philosopher

Abdera
Democritus
Protagoras
philosophers

3
4 Athens

Chaeronea
Plutarch
biographer

Cyrene

SPAIN

Marcus Aurelius
*philosopher, born
in Rome*

Uccubi

3 Eleusis
Aeschylus
tragedian
4 Megara
Theognis
poet

Callimachus *poet*
Carneades *philosopher*
Eratosthenes
geographer

Sophocles, Euripides *tragedians*,
Aristophanes, Menander *comic
dramatists*, Thucydides, Xenophon
historians, Lysias, Isocrates,
Demosthenes *orators*,
Socrates, Plato *philosopher*

Paros
Archilochus
poet

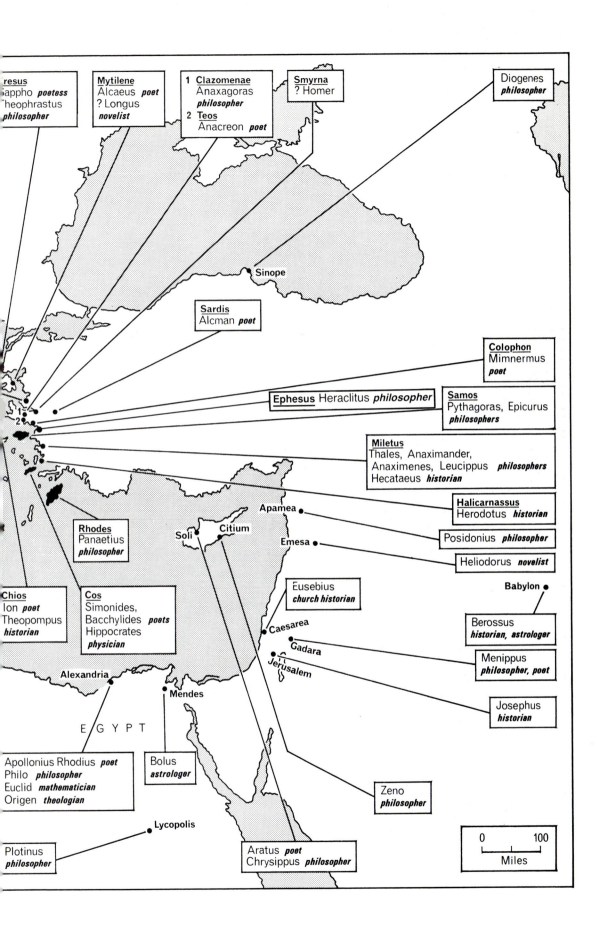

resus
Sappho *poetess*
Theophrastus
philosopher

Mytilene
Alcaeus *poet*
? Longus *novelist*

1 **Clazomenae**
Anaxagoras
philosopher
2 **Teos**
Anacreon *poet*

Smyrna
? Homer

Diogenes
philosopher

Sinope

Sardis
Alcman *poet*

Colophon
Mimnermus
poet

Ephesus Heraclitus *philosopher*

Samos
Pythagoras, Epicurus
philosophers

Miletus
Thales, Anaximander,
Anaximenes, Leucippus *philosophers*
Hecataeus *historian*

Apamea

Halicarnassus
Herodotus *historian*

Citium

Soli

Emesa

Posidonius *philosopher*

Heliodorus *novelist*

Rhodes
Panaetius
philosopher

Chios
Ion *poet*
Theopompus
historian

Cos
Simonides,
Bacchylides *poets*
Hippocrates
physician

Eusebius
church historian

Babylon

Berossus
historian, astrologer

Caesarea

Gadara

Jerusalem

Menippus
philosopher, poet

Alexandria

Mendes

Josephus
historian

E G Y P T

Apollonius Rhodius *poet*
Philo *philosopher*
Euclid *mathematician*
Origen *theologian*

Bolus
astrologer

Zeno
philosopher

Lycopolis

Plotinus
philosopher

Aratus *poet*
Chrysippus *philosopher*

0   100
Miles

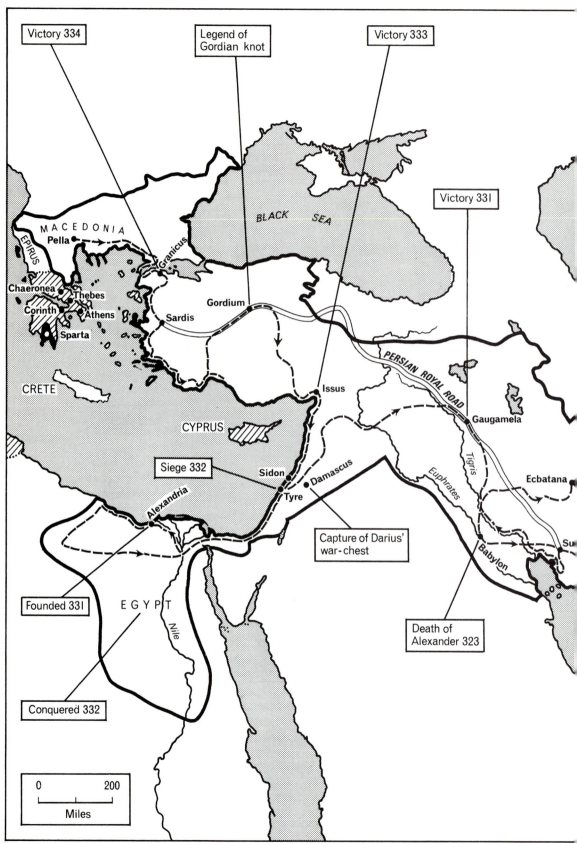

Victory 334

Legend of
Gordian knot

Victory 333

Victory 331

BLACK SEA

MACEDONIA

EPIRUS

Pella

Granicus

Chaeronea

Thebes

Corinth

Athens

Sparta

Sardis

Gordium

CRETE

CYPRUS

Issus

PERSIAN ROYAL ROAD

Gaugamela

Ecbatana

Siege 332

Sidon

Damascus

Capture of Darius'
war-chest

Tyre

Euphrates

Tigris

Babylon

Su

Alexandria

Death of
Alexander 323

Founded 331

EGYPT

Nile

Conquered 332

0   200

Miles

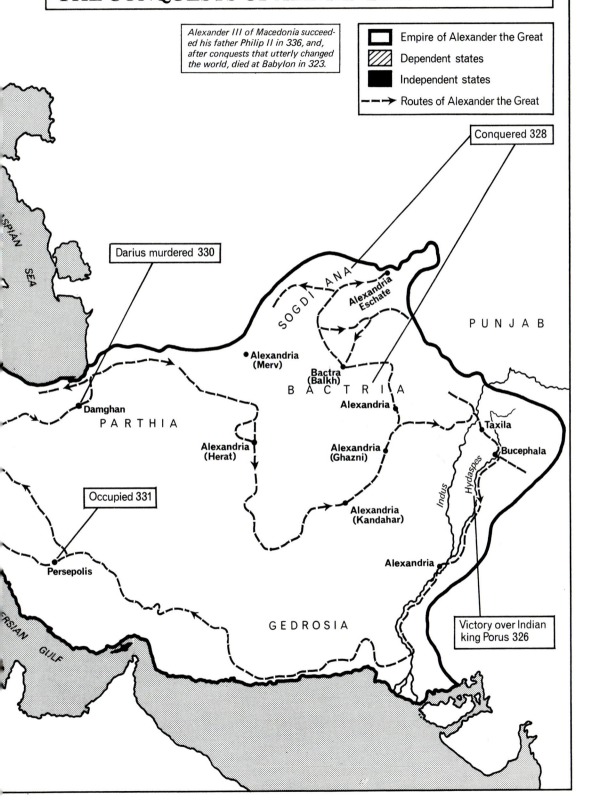

THE CONQUESTS OF ALEXANDER THE GREAT

Alexander III of Macedonia succeeded his father Philip II in 336, and, after conquests that utterly changed the world, died at Babylon in 323.

Empire of Alexander the Great
Dependent states
Independent states
- - - → Routes of Alexander the Great

Conquered 328

Darius murdered 330

SOGDIANA

Alexandria Eschate

PUNJAB

CASPIAN SEA

•Alexandria (Merv)

Bactra (Balkh)

BACTRIA

Alexandria

•Damghan

PARTHIA

Alexandria (Herat)

Alexandria (Ghazni)

Taxila

Bucephala

Indus

Hydaspes

Occupied 331

Alexandria (Kandahar)

Alexandria

Persepolis

PERSIAN GULF

GEDROSIA

Victory over Indian king Porus 326

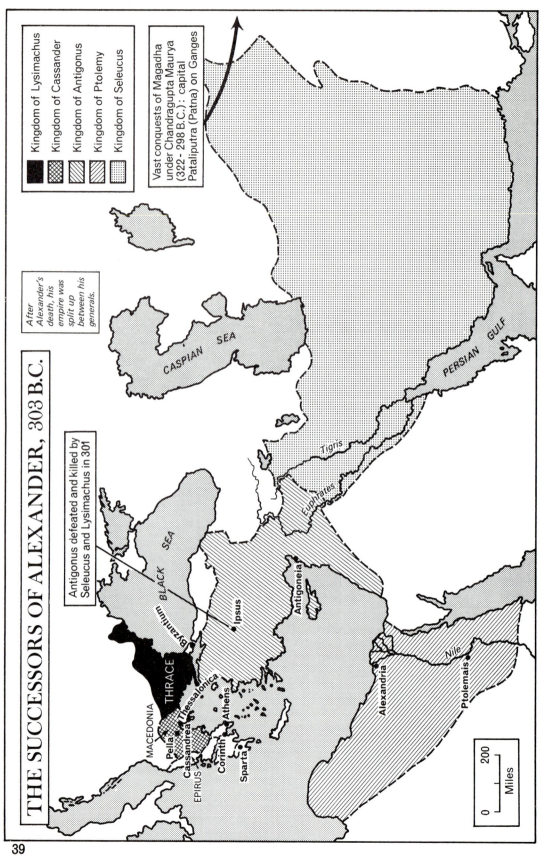

THE SUCCESSORS OF ALEXANDER, 303 B.C.

Kingdom of Lysimachus
Kingdom of Cassander
Kingdom of Antigonus
Kingdom of Ptolemy
Kingdom of Seleucus

Vast conquests of Magadha under Chandragupta Maurya (322 – 298 B.C.): capital Pataliputra (Patna) on Ganges

After Alexander's death, his empire was split up between his generals.

Antigonus defeated and killed by Seleucus and Lysimachus in 301

CASPIAN SEA

PERSIAN GULF

Tigris

Euphrates

BLACK SEA

Byzantium

THRACE

Ipsus

Antigoneia

MACEDONIA

Pella

Thessalonica

Cassandrea

Athens

Corinth

Sparta

EPIRUS

Alexandria

Nile

Ptolemais

0   200
         Miles

39

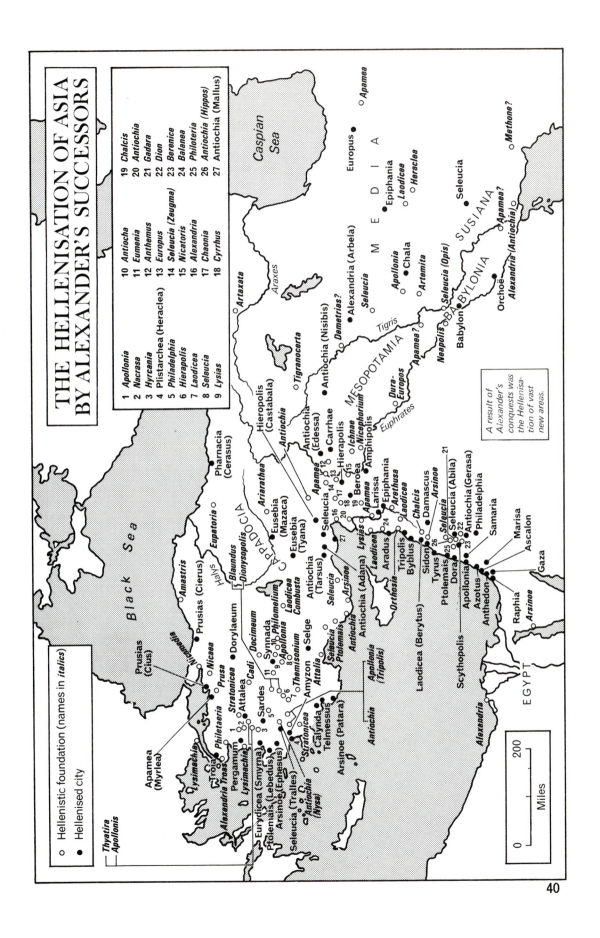

THE HELLENISATION OF ASIA
BY ALEXANDER'S SUCCESSORS

1	*Apollonia*	10	*Antiocha*
2	*Nacrasa*	11	*Eumenia*
3	*Hyrcania*	12	*Anthemus*
4	Plistarchea (Heraclea)	13	*Europus*
5	*Philadelphia*	14	*Seleucia (Zeugma)*
6	*Hierapolis*	15	*Nicatoris*
7	*Laodicea*	16	*Alexandria*
8	*Seleucia*	17	*Chaonia*
9	*Lysias*	18	*Cyrrhus*
		19	*Chalcis*
		20	*Antiochia*
		21	*Gadara*
		22	*Dion*
		23	*Berenice*
		24	*Balanea*
		25	*Philoteria*
		26	Antiochia *(Hippos)*
		27	Antiochia (Mallus)

Thyatira
Apollonis

○ Hellenistic foundation (names in *italics*)
● Hellenised city

A result of Alexander's conquests was the Hellenisation of vast new areas.

0 — 200 Miles

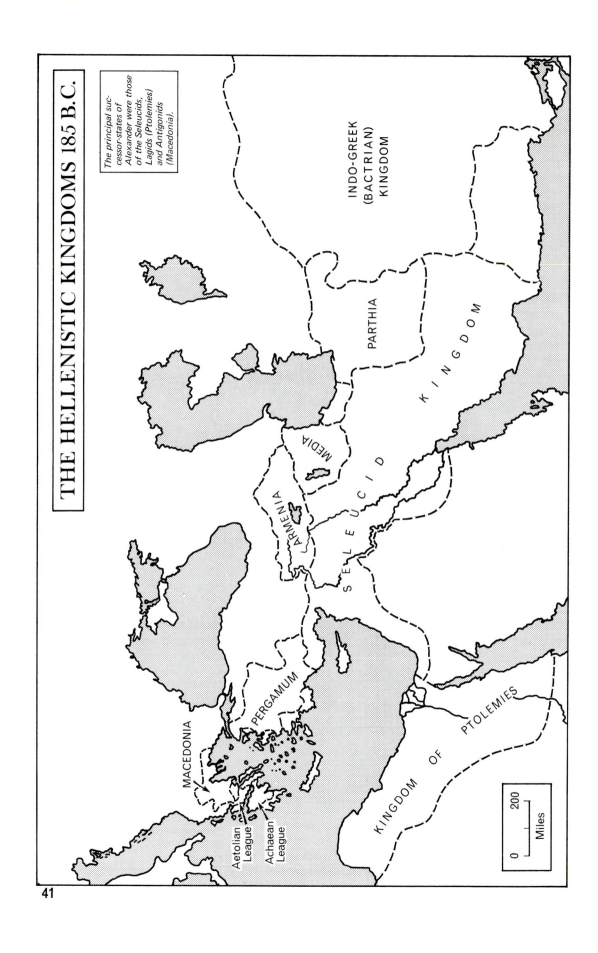

THE HELLENISTIC KINGDOMS 185 B.C.

The principal successor-states of Alexander were those of the Seleucids, Lagids (Ptolemies) and Antigonids (Macedonia).

INDO-GREEK
(BACTRIAN)
KINGDOM

PARTHIA

MEDIA

ARMENIA

S E L E U C I D   K I N G D O M

MACEDONIA

PERGAMUM

Aetolian
League

Achaean
League

KINGDOM   OF   PTOLEMIES

0   200
Miles

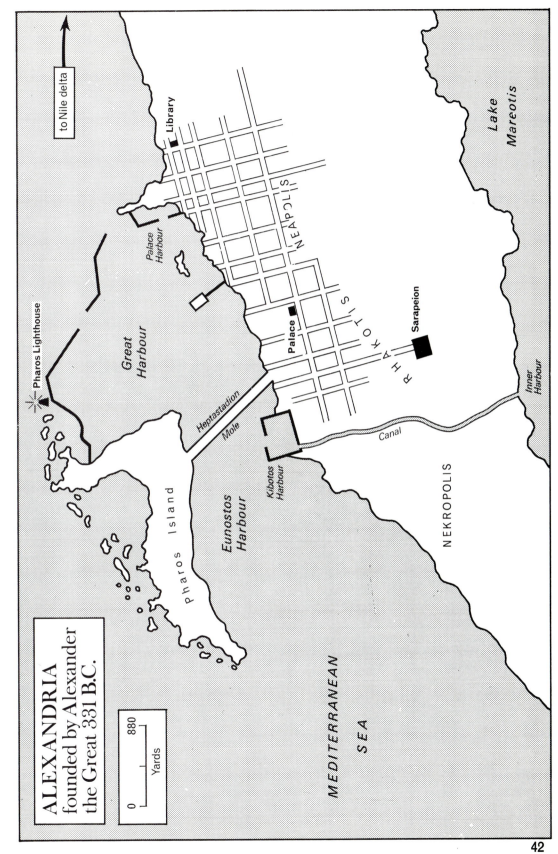

ALEXANDRIA
founded by Alexander
the Great 331 B.C.

0   880
    Yards

to Nile delta

Pharos Lighthouse

Library

Palace Harbour

Great Harbour

NEAPOLIS

Palace

RHAKOTIS

Sarapeion

Heptastadion Mole

Pharos   Island

Eunostos Harbour

Kibotos Harbour

Canal

Inner Harbour

NEKROPOLIS

MEDITERRANEAN SEA

Lake Mareotis

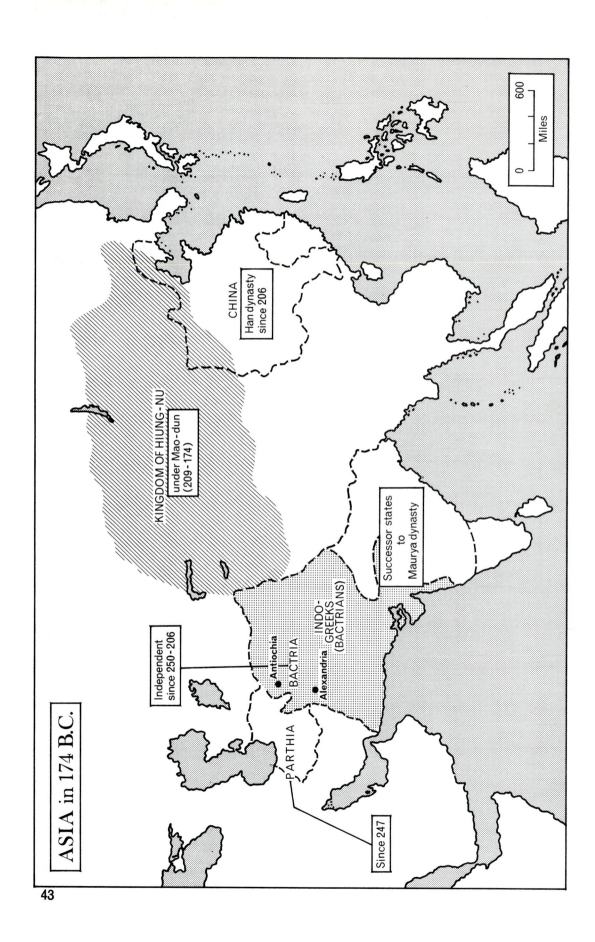

ASIA in 174 B.C.

CHINA
Han dynasty
since 206

KINGDOM OF HIUNG-NU
under Mao-dun
(209-174)

Successor states
to
Maurya dynasty

Independent
since 250-206

INDO-
GREEKS
(BACTRIANS)

Antiochia
BACTRIA
Alexandria

PARTHIA

Since 247

600
Miles
0

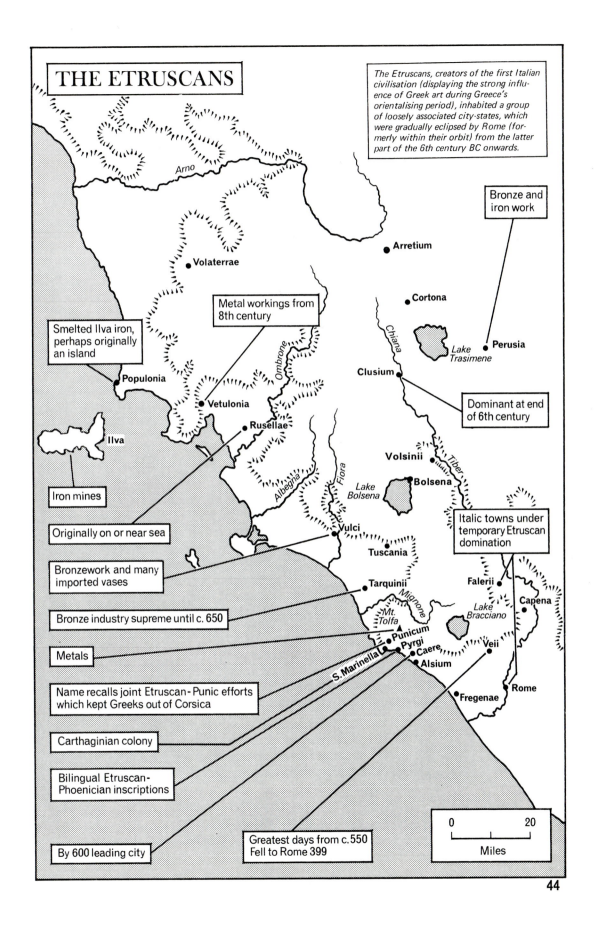

THE ETRUSCANS

The Etruscans, creators of the first Italian civilisation (displaying the strong influence of Greek art during Greece's orientalising period), inhabited a group of loosely associated city-states, which were gradually eclipsed by Rome (formerly within their orbit) from the latter part of the 6th century BC onwards.

Arno

Bronze and iron work

• **Arretium**

• **Volaterrae**

• **Cortona**

Metal workings from 8th century

Ombrone

Chiana

Smelted Ilva iron, perhaps originally an island

Lake Trasimene

• **Perusia**

• **Clusium**

Populonia

• **Vetulonia**

Dominant at end of 6th century

• **Rusellae**

Ilva

• **Volsinii**

Tiber

Iron mines

Albegna

Fiora

• **Bolsena**

Lake Bolsena

Originally on or near sea

Italic towns under temporary Etruscan domination

• **Vulci**

Bronzework and many imported vases

• **Tuscania**

• **Falerii**

Bronze industry supreme until c. 650

• **Tarquinii**

Mignone

Lake Bracciano

• **Capena**

Metals

Mt. Tolfa

▲**Punicum**

• **Pyrgi**

• **Veii**

Name recalls joint Etruscan-Punic efforts which kept Greeks out of Corsica

S. Marinella

• **Caere**

• **Alsium**

• **Rome**

Carthaginian colony

• **Fregenae**

Bilingual Etruscan-Phoenician inscriptions

0	20

Miles

By 600 leading city

Greatest days from c. 550 Fell to Rome 399

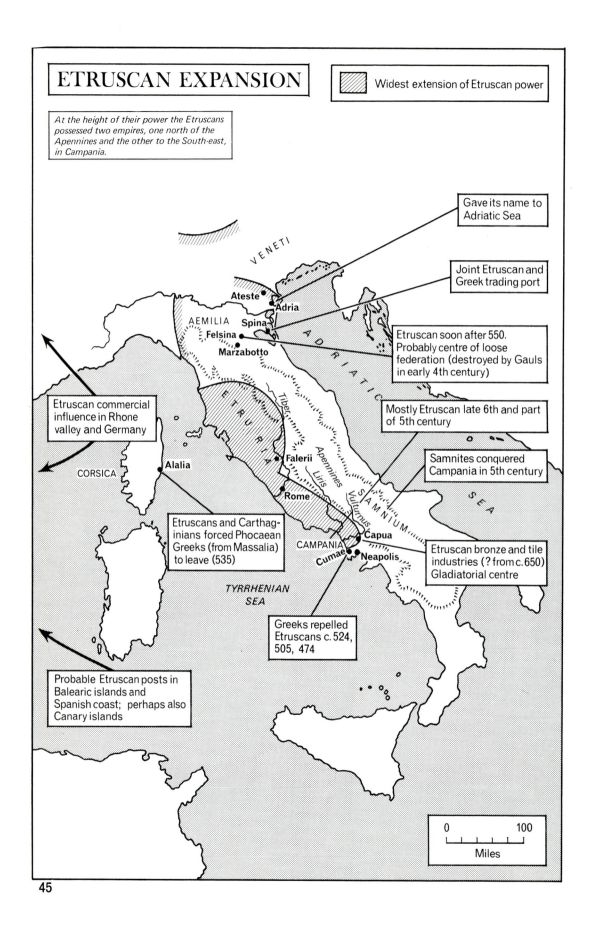

ETRUSCAN EXPANSION

Widest extension of Etruscan power

At the height of their power the Etruscans possessed two empires, one north of the Apennines and the other to the South-east, in Campania.

Gave its name to Adriatic Sea

Joint Etruscan and Greek trading port

Etruscan soon after 550. Probably centre of loose federation (destroyed by Gauls in early 4th century)

Mostly Etruscan late 6th and part of 5th century

Etruscan commercial influence in Rhone valley and Germany

Samnites conquered Campania in 5th century

Etruscans and Carthaginians forced Phocaean Greeks (from Massalia) to leave (535)

Etruscan bronze and tile industries (? from c. 650) Gladiatorial centre

Greeks repelled Etruscans c. 524, 505, 474

Probable Etruscan posts in Balearic islands and Spanish coast; perhaps also Canary islands

VENETI
Ateste
Adria
AEMILIA
Spina
Felsina
Marzabotto
ETRURIA
Tiber
ADRIATIC
CORSICA
Alalia
Falerii
Apennines
Liris
Rome
Vulturnus
SAMNIUM
SEA
Capua
CAMPANIA
Cumae
Neapolis
TYRRHENIAN SEA

0   100
Miles

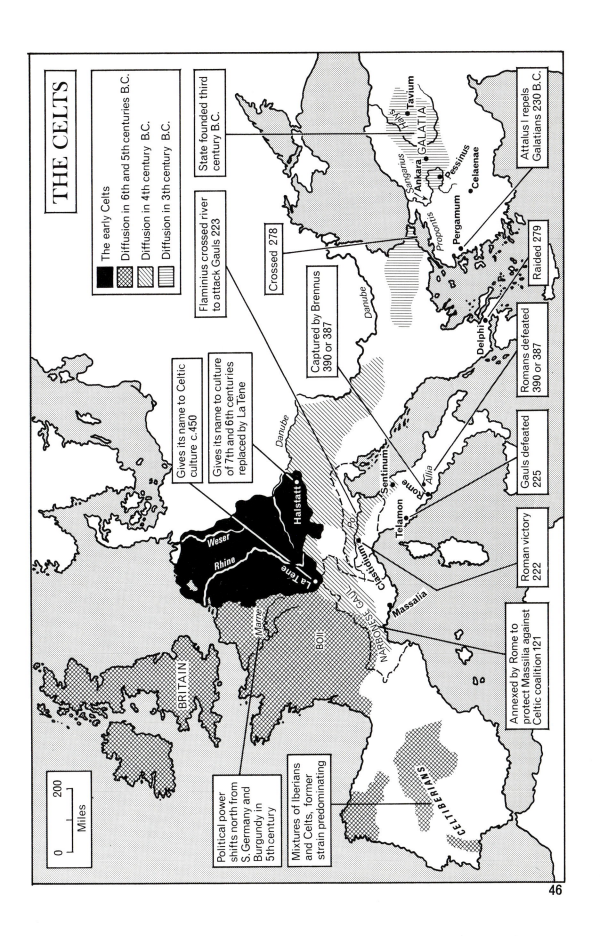

THE CELTS

Legend:
- The early Celts
- Diffusion in 6th and 5th centuries B.C.
- Diffusion in 4th century B.C.
- Diffusion in 3rd century B.C.

State founded third century B.C.

Flaminius crossed river to attack Gauls 223

Crossed 278

Attalus I repels Galatians 230 B.C.

Raided 279

Captured by Brennus 390 or 387

Romans defeated 390 or 387

Gauls defeated 225

Roman victory 222

Gives its name to Celtic culture c.450

Gives its name to culture of 7th and 6th centuries replaced by La Tène

Annexed by Rome to protect Massilia against Celtic coalition 121

Political power shifts north from S. Germany and Burgundy in 5th century

Mixtures of Iberians and Celts, former strain predominating

Labels on map: GALATIA, Tavium, Hally's, Sangarius, Ankara, Pessinus, Celaenae, Pergamum, Propontis, Delphi, Danube, Halstatt, Weser, Rhine, La Tène, Sentinum, Rome, Allia, Clastidium, Po, Telamon, BOII, CISALPINE GAUL, Massilia, NARBONNESE GAUL, Marne, BRITAIN, CELTIBERIANS

Miles: 0 — 200

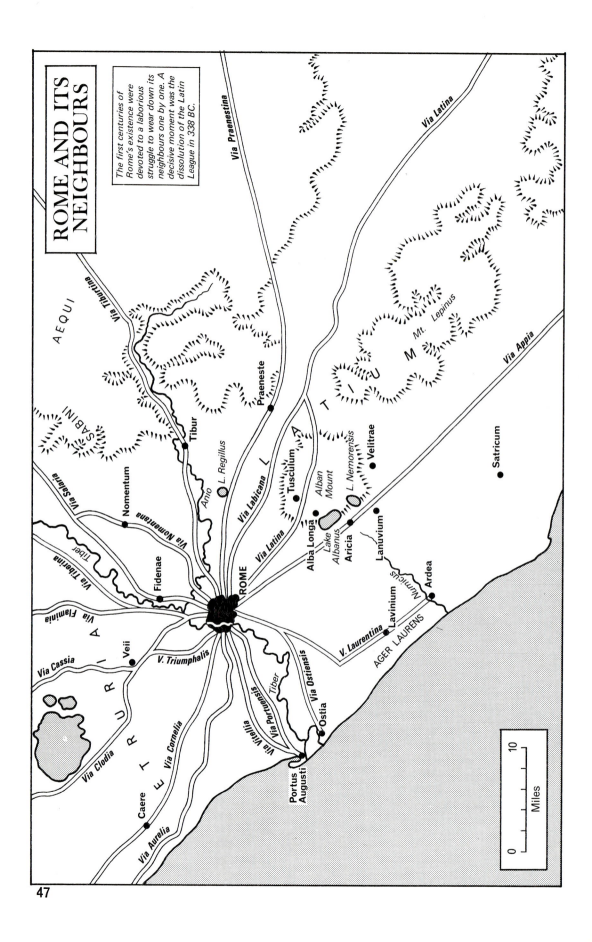

ROME AND ITS NEIGHBOURS

The first centuries of Rome's existence were devoted to a laborious struggle to wear down its neighbours one by one. A decisive moment was the dissolution of the Latin League in 338 BC.

AEQUI

Via Tiburtina

Via Praenestina

Via Latina

SABINI

Mt. Lepinus

Praeneste

Tibur

M

Via Appia

Anio

L. Regillus

Via Salaria

Nomentum

Via Labicana

Tusculum

Velitrae

Via Nomentana

Via Latina

L. Nemorensis

Satricum

Fidenae

Alban Mount

Via Tiberina

Tiber

Alba Longa

Aricia

Lanuvium

Via Flaminia

Via Cassia

Veii

ROME

V. Triumphalis

Lake Albanus

Lavinium

Ardea

Numicus

V. Laurentina

Tiber

AGER LAURENS

Vitellia

Via Ostiensis

Via Portuensis

Via Clodia

Via Cornelia

Caere

E T R U R I A

Ostia

Portus Augusti

Via Aurelia

Miles

0   10

47

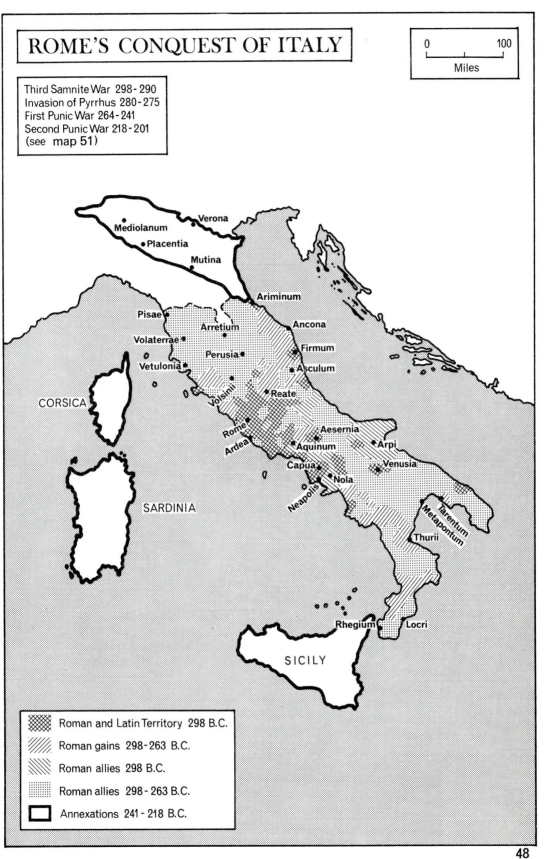

ROME'S CONQUEST OF ITALY

0 ___ 100
Miles

Third Samnite War 298-290
Invasion of Pyrrhus 280-275
First Punic War 264-241
Second Punic War 218-201
(see map 51)

Verona
Mediolanum
Placentia
Mutina
Ariminum
Pisae
Arretium
Ancona
Volaterrae
Perusia
Firmum
Vetulonia
Asculum
Volsinii
Reate
CORSICA
Rome
Aesernia
Ardea
Arpi
Aquinum
Capua
Venusia
Nola
SARDINIA
Neapolis
Tarentum
Metapontum
Thurii
Rhegium
Locri
SICILY

▨ Roman and Latin Territory 298 B.C.
▧ Roman gains 298-263 B.C.
▨ Roman allies 298 B.C.
▦ Roman allies 298-263 B.C.
▢ Annexations 241-218 B.C.

48

THE ROADS OF ROMAN ITALY

0 — 100
Miles

Augusta Praetoria
Mediolanum
Segusio
Verona ⑥ **Aquileia**
Placentia **Cremona** ①
Dertona ⑥ **Mantua**
Genua ① **Ravenna**
⑧ **Po**
Luna **Florentia** **Ariminum**
Pisae **Fanum Fortunae**
Vada Volaterrana **Arretium**
⑪ ④ **Truentum**
③ ⑬ **Aternum**
Reate
Tibur ⑦ **Corfinium**
ROME **Anagnia**
② ⑤ **Fregellae** **Beneventum** **Canusium**
Tarracina **Capua** ⑩
Cales **Casilinum** **Venusia** ② **Brundisium**
Neapolis ⑫ **Tarentum**
⑨
Rhegium

CORSICA

ADRIATIC SEA

SARDINIA

TYRRHENIAN SEA

SICILY

① Via Aemilia (187 B.C.)   ⑧ Via Julia Augusta
② Via Appia (312 - 244 B.C.)   ⑨ Via Domitiana
③ Via Aurelia   ⑩ Via Trajana
④ Via Flaminia (220 B.C.)   ⑪ Via Cassia
⑤ Via Latina   ⑫ Via Popillia
⑥ Via Postumia (148 B.C.)   ⑬ Via Salaria
⑦ Via Valeria

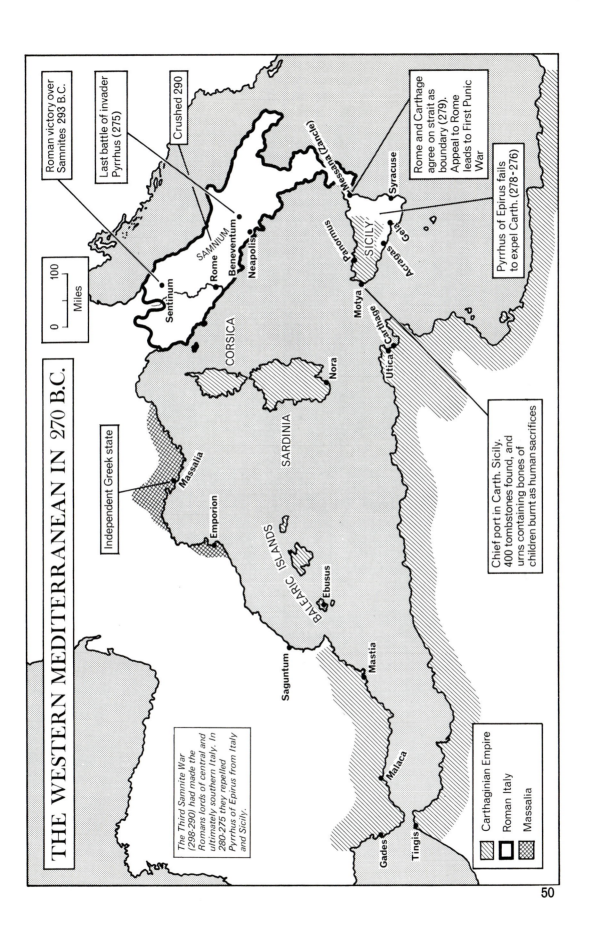

THE WESTERN MEDITERRANEAN IN 270 B.C.

The Third Samnite War (298-290) had made the Romans lords of central and ultimately southern Italy. In 280-275 they repelled Pyrrhus of Epirus from Italy and Sicily.

Roman victory over Samnites 293 B.C.

Last battle of invader Pyrrhus (275)

Crushed 290

Rome and Carthage agree on strait as boundary (279). Appeal to Rome leads to First Punic War

Pyrrhus of Epirus fails to expel Carth. (278-276)

Chief port in Carth. Sicily. 400 tombstones found, and urns containing bones of children burnt as human sacrifices

Independent Greek state

100

0

Miles

Messana (Zancle)

Syracuse

SICILY

Gela

Acragas

Panormus

Motya

Rome

Beneventum

Neapolis

SAMNIUM

Sentinum

CORSICA

SARDINIA

Nora

Utica

Carthage

Massalia

Emporion

BALEARIC ISLANDS

Ebusus

Saguntum

Mastia

Malaca

Gades

Tingis

Carthaginian Empire

Roman Italy

Massalia

50

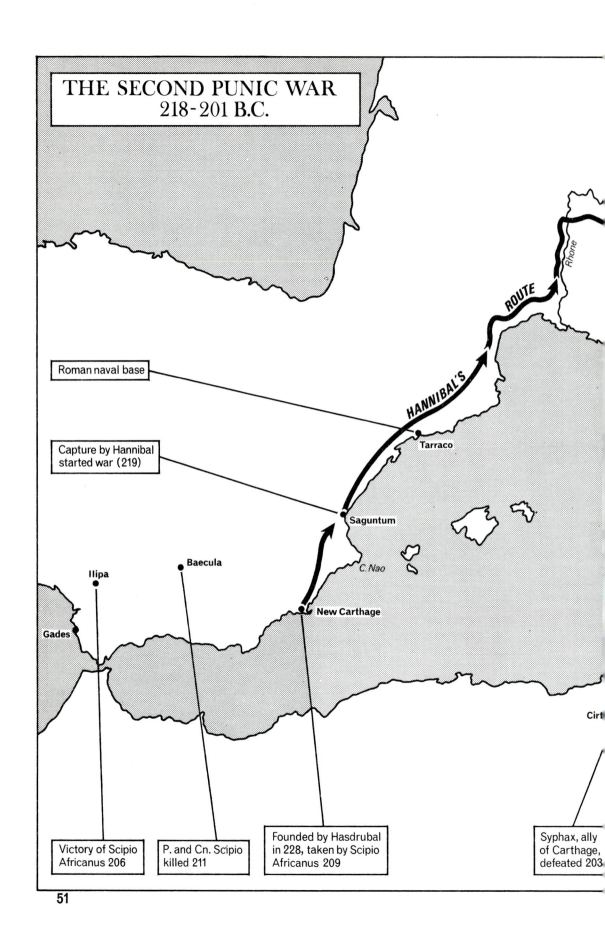

THE SECOND PUNIC WAR
218-201 B.C.

Roman naval base

Capture by Hannibal started war (219)

HANNIBAL'S ROUTE

Rhone

Tarraco

Saguntum

C. Nao

Baecula

Ilipa

Gades

New Carthage

Cirt

Victory of Scipio Africanus 206

P. and Cn. Scipio killed 211

Founded by Hasdrubal in 228, taken by Scipio Africanus 209

Syphax, ally of Carthage, defeated 203

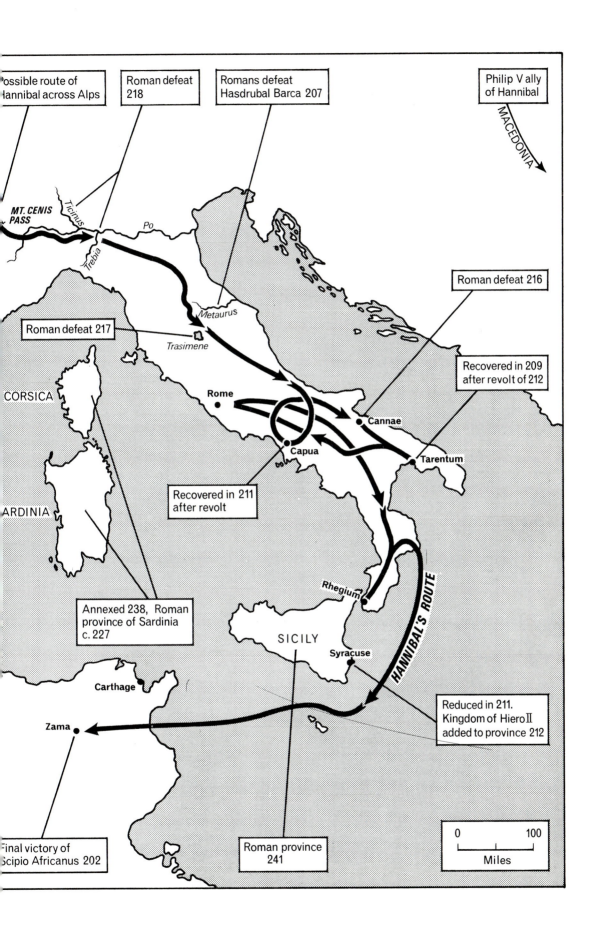

Possible route of Hannibal across Alps

Roman defeat 218

Romans defeat Hasdrubal Barca 207

Philip V ally of Hannibal

MACEDONIA

MT. CENIS PASS

Ticinus

Po

Trebia

Metaurus

Roman defeat 216

Roman defeat 217

Trasimene

CORSICA

Rome

Recovered in 209 after revolt of 212

Cannae

Capua

Tarentum

Recovered in 211 after revolt

SARDINIA

Annexed 238, Roman province of Sardinia c. 227

Rhegium

HANNIBAL'S ROUTE

SICILY

Carthage

Syracuse

Zama

Reduced in 211. Kingdom of Hiero II added to province 212

Final victory of Scipio Africanus 202

Roman province 241

0   100

Miles

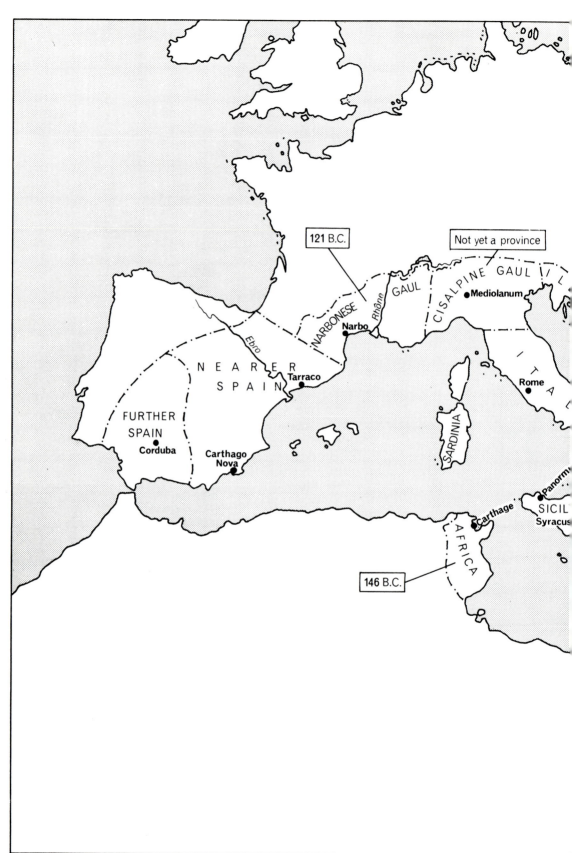

121 B.C.

Not yet a province

CISALPINE GAUL

GAUL

Rhône

●Mediolanum

NARBONESE

Narbo●

N E A R E R
S P A I N

Tarraco●

Ebro

Rome●

FURTHER
SPAIN

SARDINIA

Corduba●

Carthago
Nova●

Panorm●

SICIL

Syracus●

●Carthage

A F R I C A

146 B.C.

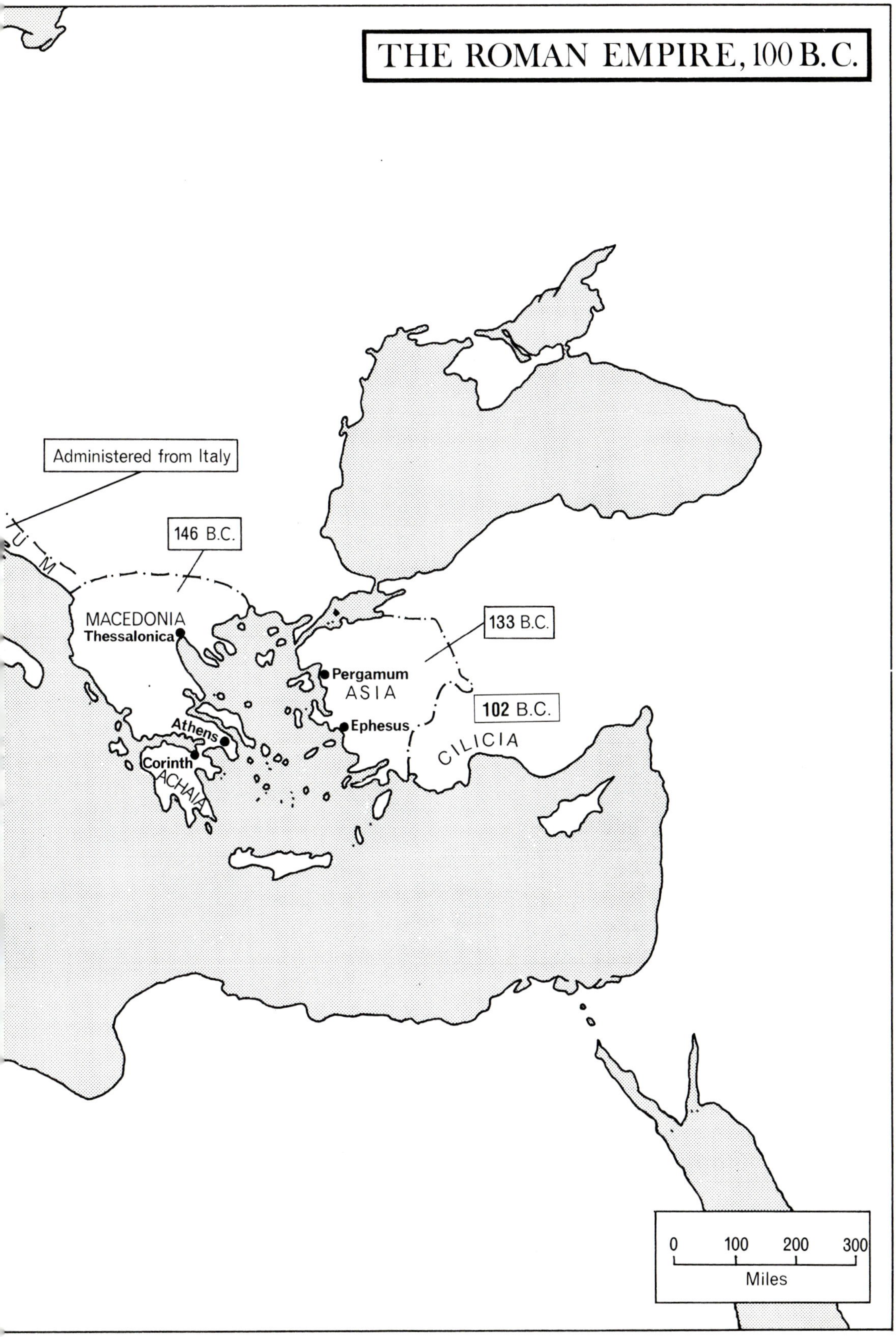

THE ROMAN EMPIRE, 100 B.C.

Administered from Italy

146 B.C.

133 B.C.

102 B.C.

U — M —

MACEDONIA
Thessalonica

Pergamum
ASIA

Athens

Ephesus

CILICIA

Corinth
ACHAIA

0   100   200   300
Miles

BRITANNIA

GAUL
(GALLIA COMATA)

Conquered by
Caesar 58-51 B.C.

Rhine

Citizenship granted 49
province 42 B.C.

Lugdunum

CISALPINE GAUL

Mediolanum

Rhône

GAUL

NARBONESE

Narbo

Massilia

Rubicon

ILLYRI...

Ebro

Ilerda

Tarraco

ITALY

Rome

FURTHER
SPAIN

NEARER
SPAIN

SARDINIA

Cordoba

Munda

Panormus

Carthage

Syracuse

SICILY

Cirta

AFRICA
NOVA

AFRICA

Thapsus

Province 46-30 B.C.

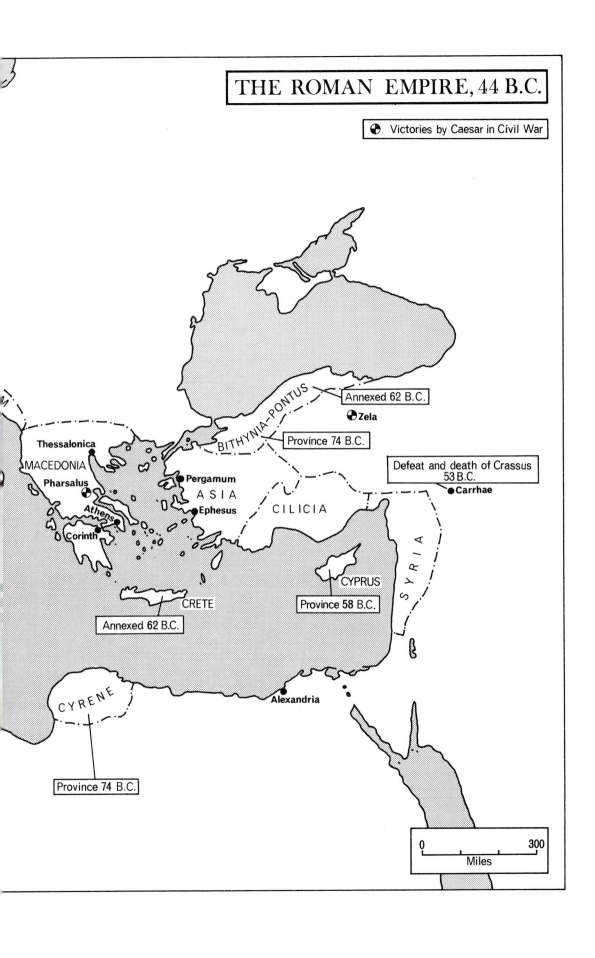

THE ROMAN EMPIRE, 44 B.C.

◓ Victories by Caesar in Civil War

Annexed 62 B.C.

◓ **Zela**

BITHYNIA-PONTUS

Province 74 B.C.

Defeat and death of Crassus
53 B.C.

● **Carrhae**

Thessalonica

MACEDONIA

Pharsalus

Pergamum

A S I A

C I L I C I A

Ephesus

Athens

Corinth

S Y R I A

CYPRUS

CRETE

Province 58 B.C.

Annexed 62 B.C.

C Y R E N E

Alexandria

Province 74 B.C.

0   300
Miles

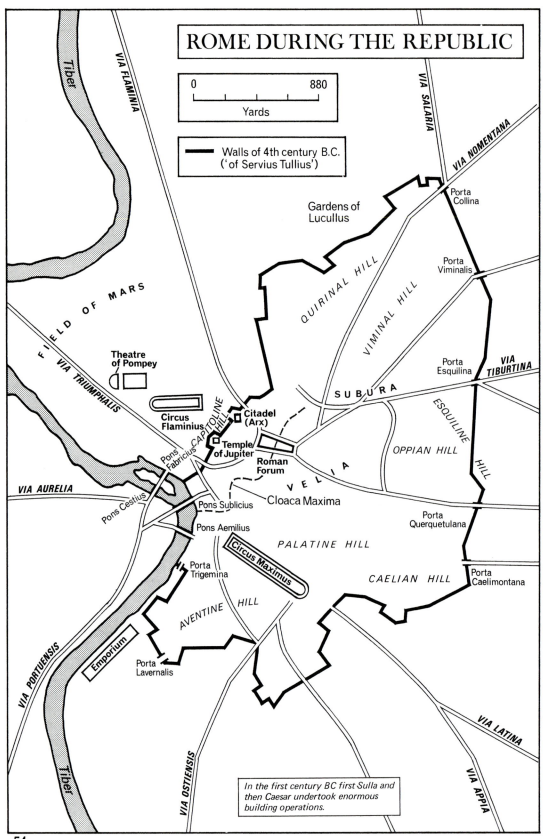

ROME DURING THE REPUBLIC

0   880

Yards

▬▬▬ Walls of 4th century B.C.
('of Servius Tullius')

Tiber

VIA FLAMINIA

VIA SALARIA

VIA NOMENTANA

Porta
Collina

Gardens of
Lucullus

QUIRINAL HILL

VIMINAL HILL

Porta
Viminalis

FIELD OF MARS

VIA TRIUMPHALIS

Theatre
of Pompey

Porta
Esquilina

VIA
TIBURTINA

SUBURA

Circus
Flaminius

CAPITOLINE HILL

Citadel
(Arx)

ESQUILINE HILL

OPPIAN HILL

Pons
Fabricius

Temple
of Jupiter

Roman
Forum

VELIA

VIA AURELIA

Pons Cestius

Pons Sublicius

Cloaca Maxima

Porta
Querquetulana

Pons Aemilius

PALATINE HILL

Porta
Trigemina

Circus Maximus

CAELIAN HILL

Porta
Caelimontana

VIA PORTUENSIS

Emporium

AVENTINE HILL

Porta
Lavernalis

VIA OSTIENSIS

VIA LATINA

VIA APPIA

In the first century BC first Sulla and
then Caesar undertook enormous
building operations.

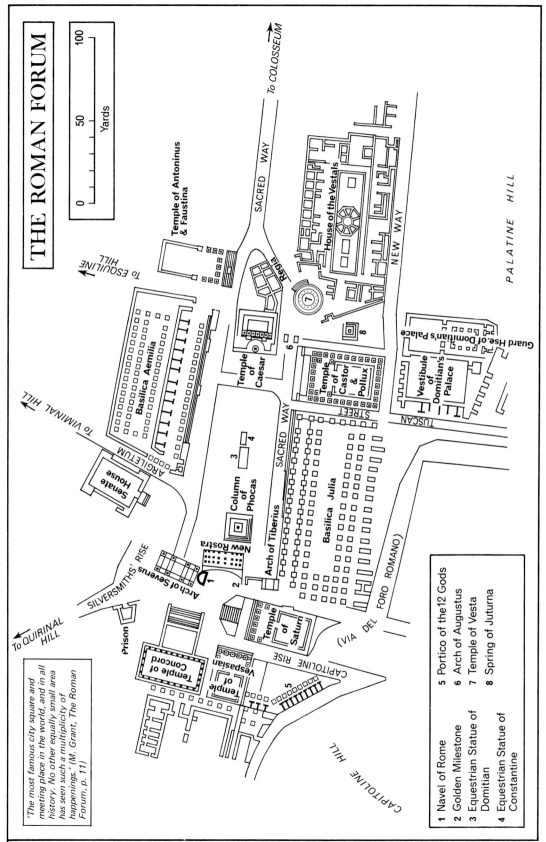

THE ROMAN FORUM

Yards
0   50   100

'The most famous city square and meeting place in the world, and in all history. No other equally small area has seen such a multiplicity of happenings.' (M. Grant, The Roman Forum, p. 11)

Temple of Antoninus & Faustina

To ESQUILINE HILL

SACRED WAY

To COLOSSEUM

Regia

House of the Vestals

NEW WAY

PALATINE HILL

7

8

Guard Hse. of Domitian's Palace

Temple of Caesar

6

Basilica Aemilia

To VIMINAL HILL

Temple of Castor & Pollux

Vestibule of Domitian's Palace

TUSCAN STREET

Senate House

ARGILETUM

3
4

Column of Phocas

SACRED WAY

Basilica Julia

To QUIRINAL HILL

SILVERSMITHS' RISE

New Rostra

Arch of Tiberius

1
Arch of Severus

2

(VIA DEL FORO ROMANO)

Prison

Temple of Saturn

CAPITOLINE RISE

Temple of Concord

Temple of Vespasian

5

CAPITOLINE HILL

1 Navel of Rome
2 Golden Milestone
3 Equestrian Statue of Domitian
4 Equestrian Statue of Constantine
5 Portico of the 12 Gods
6 Arch of Augustus
7 Temple of Vesta
8 Spring of Juturna

55

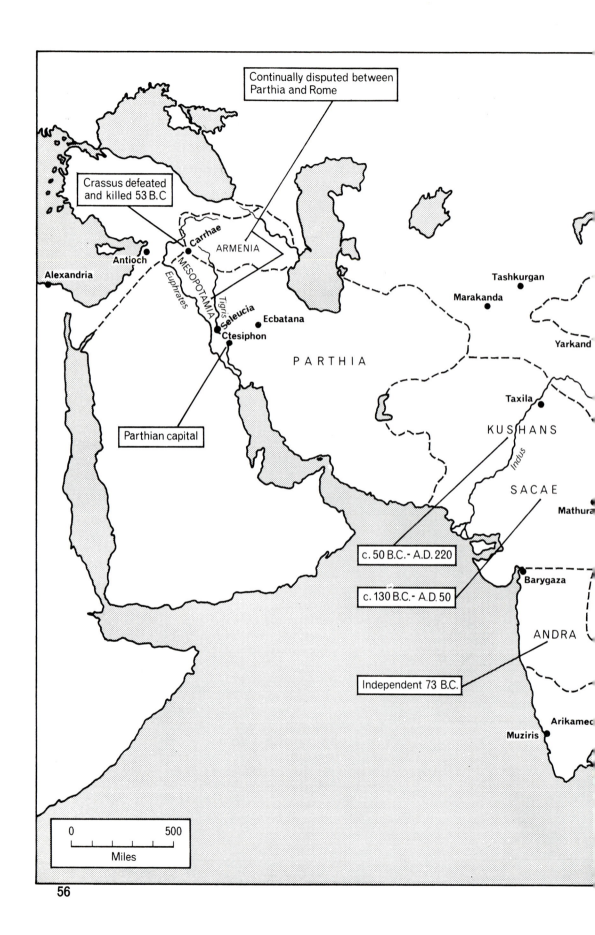

Continually disputed between
Parthia and Rome

Crassus defeated
and killed 53 B.C

Carrhae

ARMENIA

Antioch

Alexandria

MESOPOTAMIA

Euphrates

Tigris

Seleucia

Ecbatana

Ctesiphon

PARTHIA

Tashkurgan

Marakanda

Yarkand

Parthian capital

Taxila

KUSHANS

Indus

SACAE

Mathura

c. 50 B.C.- A.D. 220

c. 130 B.C.- A.D. 50

Barygaza

ANDRA

Independent 73 B.C.

Arikamed

Muziris

0   500

Miles

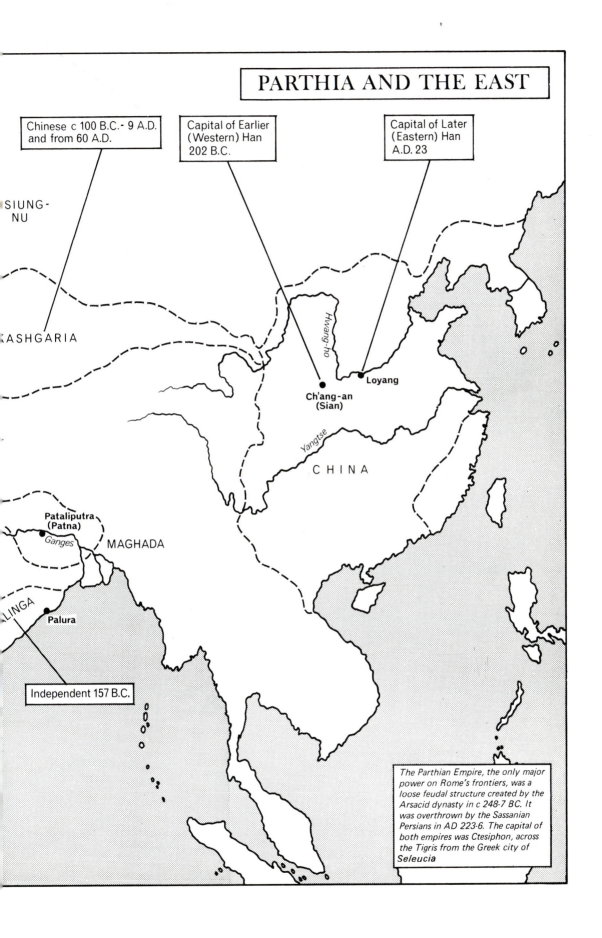

PARTHIA AND THE EAST

Chinese c 100 B.C.- 9 A.D. and from 60 A.D.

Capital of Earlier (Western) Han 202 B.C.

Capital of Later (Eastern) Han A.D. 23

SIUNG-NU

KASHGARIA

Hwang-ho

Loyang

Ch'ang-an (Sian)

Yangtse

C H I N A

Pataliputra (Patna)

Ganges

MAGHADA

LINGA

Palura

Independent 157 B.C.

The Parthian Empire, the only major power on Rome's frontiers, was a loose feudal structure created by the Arsacid dynasty in c 248-7 BC. It was overthrown by the Sassanian Persians in AD 223-6. The capital of both empires was Ctesiphon, across the Tigris from the Greek city of *Seleucia*

BRITANNIA

FREE GERMANY

LWR. GERMANY (17 B.C.)

Temporarily conquered from 15 B.C. but abandoned after ambushing of Varus by Arminius in A.D. 9

Colonia Agrippinensis

Moguntiacum

Rhine

BELGICA

Danube

LOWER PANNONIA (10 B.C.)

LUGDUNENSIS

UPR. GERMANY (17 B.C.)

RHAETIA (15 B.C.)

NORICUM (15 B.C.)

UPPER PANNONIA

Lugdunum

P

Aquileia

AQUITANIA

NARBONENSIS

C

M

I T A L Y

Adriatic Sea

Nemausus

Rome

TARRACONENSIS

Tarraco

LUSITANIA (c. 27 B.C.)

Naulochus

SICILY

Corduba

BAETICA

Carthage

Gades

Naval victory over Sextus Pompeius 36 B.C.

M A U R E T A N I A

A F R I C A

──────── Imperial frontier as in A.D. 14

- - - - - - Provincial frontiers

ASIA   Senatorial provinces

ALPINE PROVINCES (15-14 B.C.)
M: Maritime, C: Cottian, P: Pennine

The hatched areas represent the more important dependent ('client') states, whose monarchs enjoyed internal autonomy but had to support Rome's foreign policy and help defend the imperial frontiers.

//// Principal client states

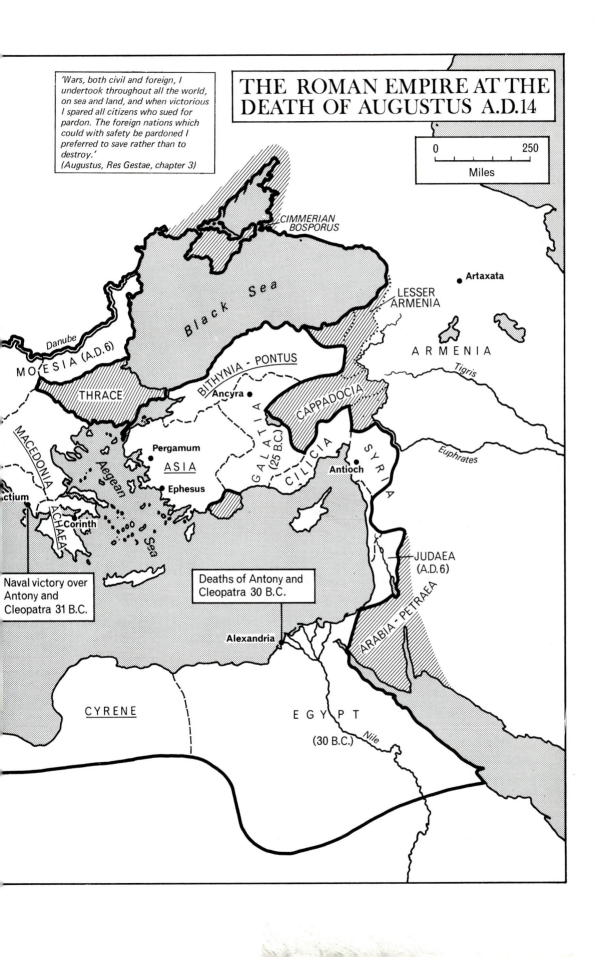

THE ROMAN EMPIRE AT THE DEATH OF AUGUSTUS A.D. 14

0   250

Miles

CIMMERIAN
BOSPORUS

Artaxata

LESSER
ARMENIA

ARMENIA

Black Sea

Danube

Tigris

MOESIA (A.D. 6)

BITHYNIA - PONTUS

THRACE

Ancyra

CAPPADOCIA

MACEDONIA

Pergamum

GALATIA
(25 B.C.)

CILICIA

SYRIA

Euphrates

ASIA

Antioch

Aegean

Ephesus

ctium

ACHAEA

Corinth

Sea

JUDAEA
(A.D. 6)

Naval victory over
Antony and
Cleopatra 31 B.C.

Deaths of Antony and
Cleopatra 30 B.C.

ARABIA - PETRAEA

Alexandria

CYRENE

E G Y P T

(30 B.C.)

Nile

Imperial frontier as in A.D. 14

Roman roads

Mountain contours

All roads lead to Rome: the most
potent guarantees of external and
internal peace and stimulants of
prosperity.

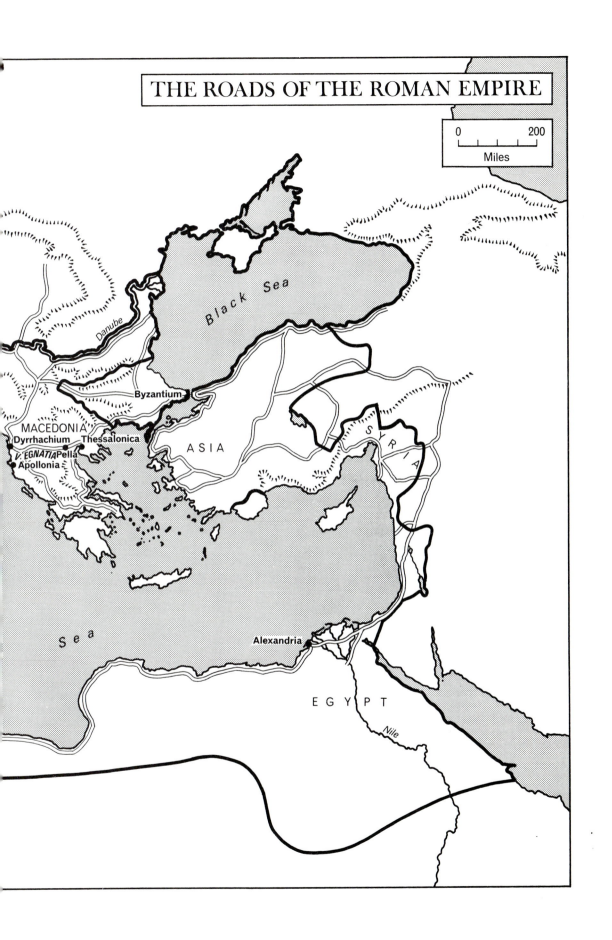

THE ROADS OF THE ROMAN EMPIRE

Miles

0   200

Black Sea

Danube

Byzantium

MACEDONIA
Dyrrhachium   **Thessalonica**
*V. EGNATIA***Pella**
Apollonia

A S I A

S Y R I A

Sea

Alexandria

E G Y P T

Nile

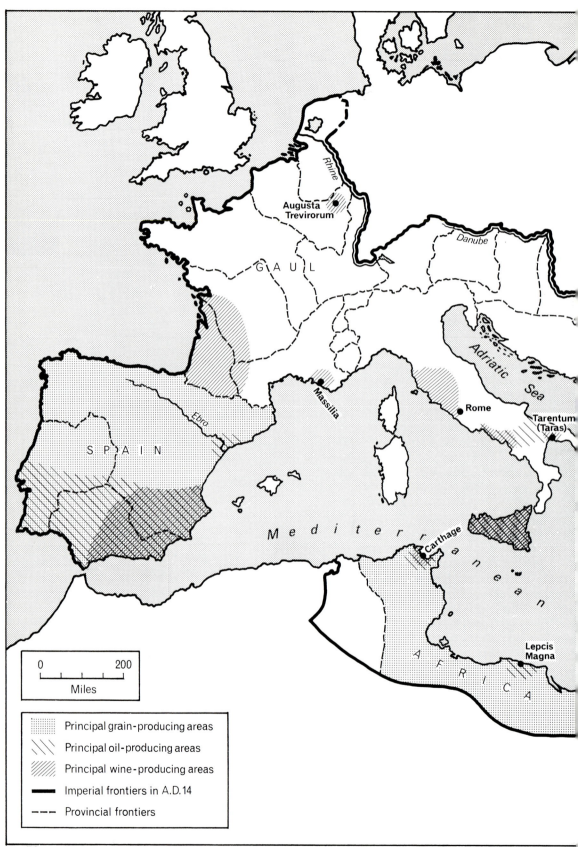

Augusta
Trevirorum

Rhine

GAUL

Danube

Adriatic

Ebro

SPAIN

Massilia

Rome

Tarentum
(Taras)

Sea

Mediterr

anean

Carthage

AFRICA

Lepcis
Magna

0   200

Miles

Principal grain-producing areas

Principal oil-producing areas

Principal wine-producing areas

Imperial frontiers in A.D.14

Provincial frontiers

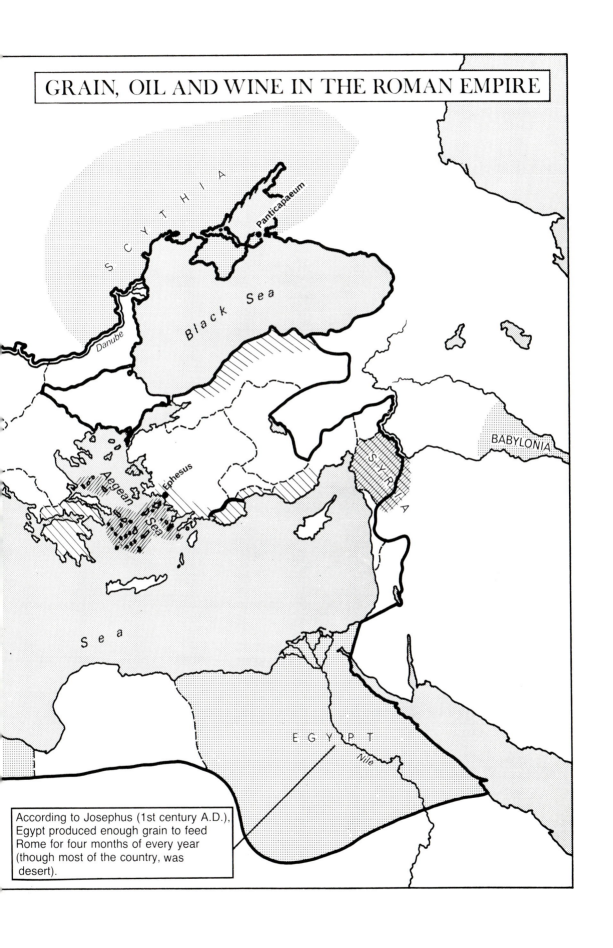

GRAIN, OIL AND WINE IN THE ROMAN EMPIRE

S C Y T H I A

Panticapaeum

Black Sea

Danube

BABYLONIA

Aegean Sea

Ephesus

S Y R I A

Sea

E G Y P T

Nile

According to Josephus (1st century A.D.),
Egypt produced enough grain to feed
Rome for four months of every year
(though most of the country, was
desert).

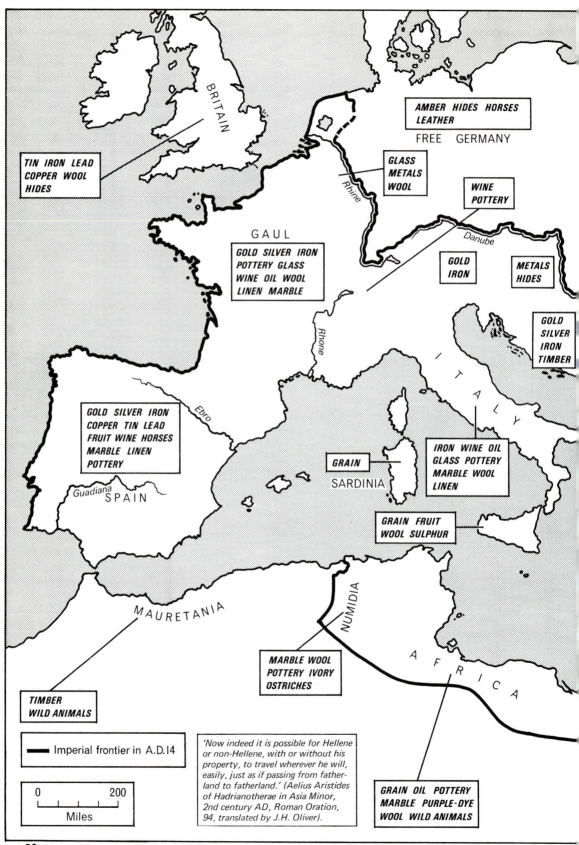

BRITAIN

TIN IRON LEAD
COPPER WOOL
HIDES

FREE GERMANY

AMBER HIDES HORSES
LEATHER

Rhine

GLASS
METALS
WOOL

GAUL

GOLD SILVER IRON
POTTERY GLASS
WINE OIL WOOL
LINEN MARBLE

WINE
POTTERY

Danube

GOLD
IRON

METALS
HIDES

Rhone

GOLD
SILVER
IRON
TIMBER

I T A L Y

Ebro

GOLD SILVER IRON
COPPER TIN LEAD
FRUIT WINE HORSES
MARBLE LINEN
POTTERY

GRAIN

SARDINIA

IRON WINE OIL
GLASS POTTERY
MARBLE WOOL
LINEN

Guadiana SPAIN

GRAIN FRUIT
WOOL SULPHUR

MAURETANIA

NUMIDIA

A F R I C A

MARBLE WOOL
POTTERY IVORY
OSTRICHES

TIMBER
WILD ANIMALS

— Imperial frontier in A.D.14

'Now indeed it is possible for Hellene
or non-Hellene, with or without his
property, to travel wherever he will,
easily, just as if passing from fatherland to fatherland.' (Aelius Aristides
of Hadrianotherae in Asia Minor,
2nd century AD, Roman Oration,
94, translated by J.H. Oliver).

GRAIN OIL POTTERY
MARBLE PURPLE-DYE
WOOL WILD ANIMALS

0   200
Miles

TRADING PRODUCTS IN THE ROMAN EMPIRE

Dnieper

GRAIN HONEY HEMP
NUTS HIDES

GOLD TIMBER
HORSES SALT

Dniester

Bug

S C Y T H I A

IRON

CAUCASUS

SILK
from China

D A C I A

Black Sea

ARMENIA

IRON

GRAIN FISH GOLD
SILVER IRON LEAD

Danube

METALS BITUMEN
PRECIOUS STONES

MOESIA

THRACE

MESOPOTAMIA

Tigris

GRAIN FISH
HORSES

ASIA

MACEDONIA

WOOL LINEN WINE
OIL MARBLE POTTERY
PARCHMENT TIMBER
HORSES EMERALDS
GOLD SILVER IRON

Euphrates

SILK from China

S
Y
R
I
A

GREECE

CYPRUS

JUDAEA

WOOL PURPLE-DYE
LINEN GLASS
POTTERY TIMBER
LEATHER-GOODS

COPPER OIL

WINE HONEY LINEN
PURPLE-DYE
POTTERY
MARBLE

ARABIA

ASPHALT

FRANKINCENSE AND
OTHER PERFUMES

EGYPT

to South Arabia

CYRENE

GLASS GRAIN LINEN
TEXTILES DRUGS PAPYRUS
WILD ANIMALS PORPHYRY

PEPPER from India

IVORY from Central Africa

SILPHIUM [Medicinal
herb] TIMBER

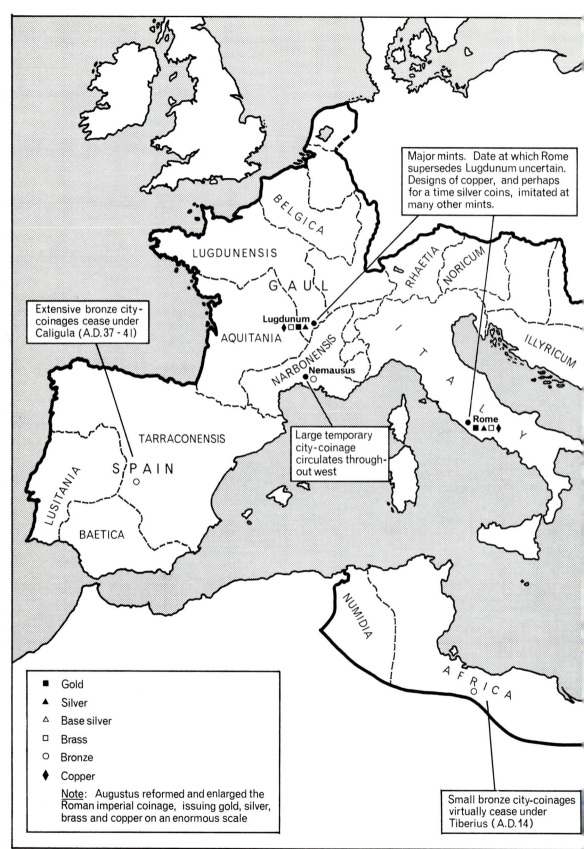

Major mints. Date at which Rome supersedes Lugdunum uncertain. Designs of copper, and perhaps for a time silver coins, imitated at many other mints.

Extensive bronze city-coinages cease under Caligula (A.D. 37 - 41)

Large temporary city-coinage circulates through-out west

BELGICA

LUGDUNENSIS

GAUL

Lugdunum

AQUITANIA

NARBONENSIS

Nemausus

RHAETIA

NORICUM

ILLYRICUM

ITALY

Rome

TARRACONENSIS

SPAIN

LUSITANIA

BAETICA

NUMIDIA

AFRICA

- ■ Gold
- ▲ Silver
- △ Base silver
- □ Brass
- ○ Bronze
- ◆ Copper

Note: Augustus reformed and enlarged the Roman imperial coinage, issuing gold, silver, brass and copper on an enormous scale

Small bronze city-coinages virtually cease under Tiberius (A.D. 14)

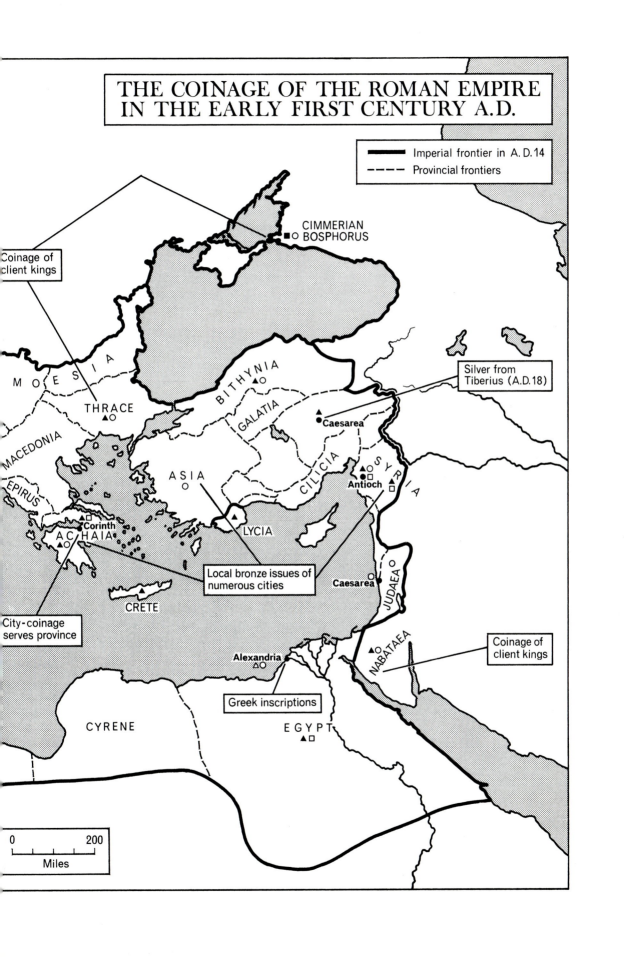

THE COINAGE OF THE ROMAN EMPIRE
IN THE EARLY FIRST CENTURY A.D.

Imperial frontier in A.D.14
Provincial frontiers

CIMMERIAN
BOSPHORUS

Coinage of
client kings

M O E S I A

THRACE

MACEDONIA

EPIRUS

BITHYNIA

GALATIA

Silver from
Tiberius (A.D.18)

Caesarea

ASIA

CILICIA

S Y R I A

Antioch

LYCIA

A C H A I A

Corinth

Local bronze issues of
numerous cities

Caesarea

JUDAEA

City-coinage
serves province

CRETE

Alexandria

Coinage of
client kings

NABATAEA

Greek inscriptions

CYRENE

E G Y P T

0   200

Miles

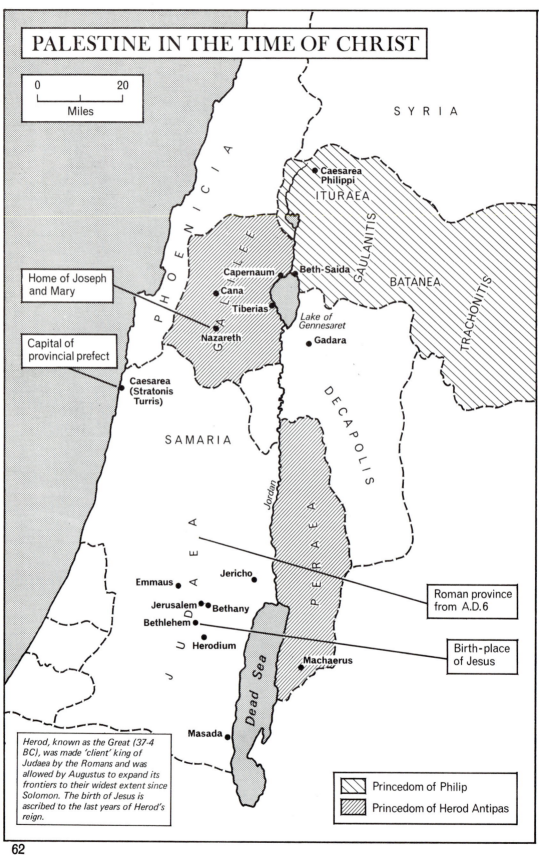

PALESTINE IN THE TIME OF CHRIST

0 — 20
Miles

SYRIA

PHOENICIA

Caesarea
Philippi

ITURAEA

GAULANITIS

BATANEA

TRACHONITIS

Home of Joseph
and Mary

Capernaum
Cana
Tiberias

Beth-Saida

GALILEE

Lake of
Gennesaret

Nazareth

Gadara

DECAPOLIS

Capital of
provincial prefect

Caesarea
(Stratonis
Turris)

SAMARIA

Jordan

PERAEA

Roman province
from A.D. 6

Emmaus

Jericho

JUDAEA

Jerusalem
Bethlehem

Bethany

Herodium

Machaerus

Birth-place
of Jesus

Dead Sea

Masada

Herod, known as the Great (37-4
BC), was made 'client' king of
Judaea by the Romans and was
allowed by Augustus to expand its
frontiers to their widest extent since
Solomon. The birth of Jesus is
ascribed to the last years of Herod's
reign.

///// Princedom of Philip
///// Princedom of Herod Antipas

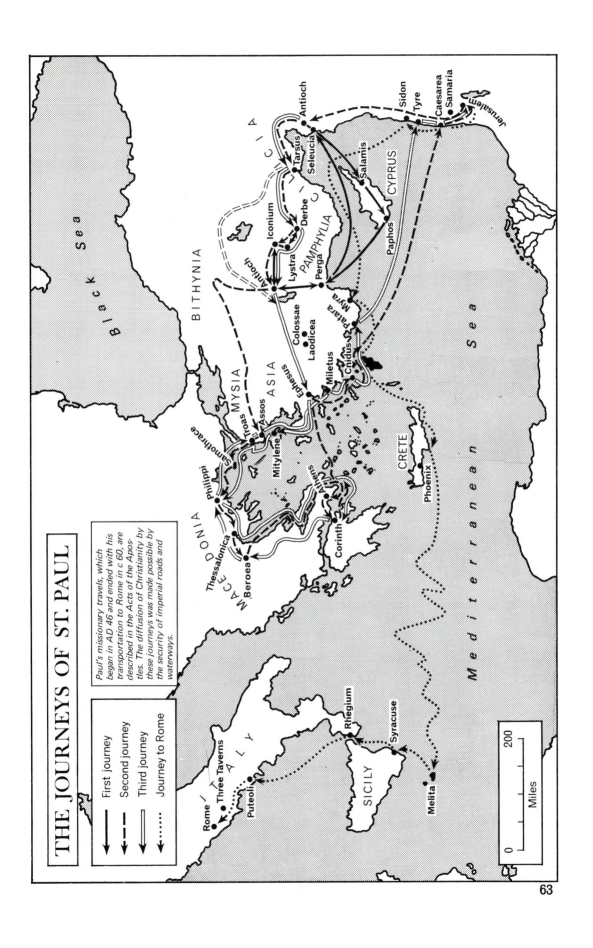

THE JOURNEYS OF ST. PAUL

First journey
Second journey
Third journey
Journey to Rome

Paul's missionary travels, which began in AD 46 and ended with his transportation to Rome in c 60, are described in the Acts of the Apostles. The diffusion of Christianity by these journeys was made possible by the security of imperial roads and waterways.

0   200
Miles

Black Sea

Mediterranean Sea

BITHYNIA

MYSIA

ASIA

MACEDONIA

CRETE

SICILY

ITALY

CYPRUS

PAMPHYLIA

CILICIA

Rome
Three Taverns
Puteoli
Rhegium
Syracuse
Melita
Phoenix
Thessalonica
Beroea
Philippi
Samothrace
Athens
Corinth
Troas
Assos
Mitylene
Ephesus
Miletus
Cnidus
Patara
Myra
Colossae
Laodicea
Antioch
Iconium
Derbe
Lystra
Perga
Tarsus
Seleucia
Salamis
Paphos
Sidon
Tyre
Caesarea
Samaria
Jerusalem

63

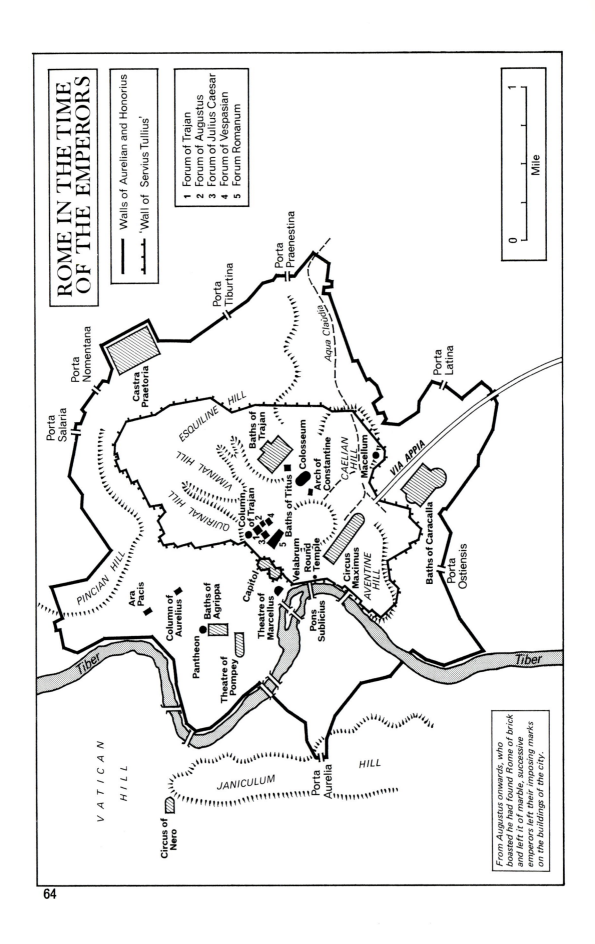

ROME IN THE TIME OF THE EMPERORS

Walls of Aurelian and Honorius
'Wall of Servius Tullius'

1 Forum of Trajan
2 Forum of Augustus
3 Forum of Julius Caesar
4 Forum of Vespasian
5 Forum Romanum

0   Mile   1

From Augustus onwards, who boasted he had found Rome of brick and left it of marble, successive emperors left their imposing marks on the buildings of the city.

Porta Praenestina
Porta Tiburtina
Porta Latina
Porta Nomentana
Castra Praetoria
Porta Salaria
Aqua Claudia
ESQUILINE HILL
Baths of Trajan
Colosseum
Macellum
Arch of Constantine
CAELIAN HILL
VIA APPIA
VIMINAL HILL
Column of Trajan
QUIRINAL HILL
Baths of Titus
Baths of Caracalla
Porta Ostiensis
Velabrum
Round Temple
Circus Maximus
AVENTINE HILL
PINCIAN HILL
Ara Pacis
Column of Aurelius
Baths of Agrippa
Pantheon
Theatre of Pompey
Capitol
Theatre of Marcellus
Pons Sublicius
Tiber
Tiber
VATICAN HILL
Circus of Nero
JANICULUM   HILL
Porta Aurelia

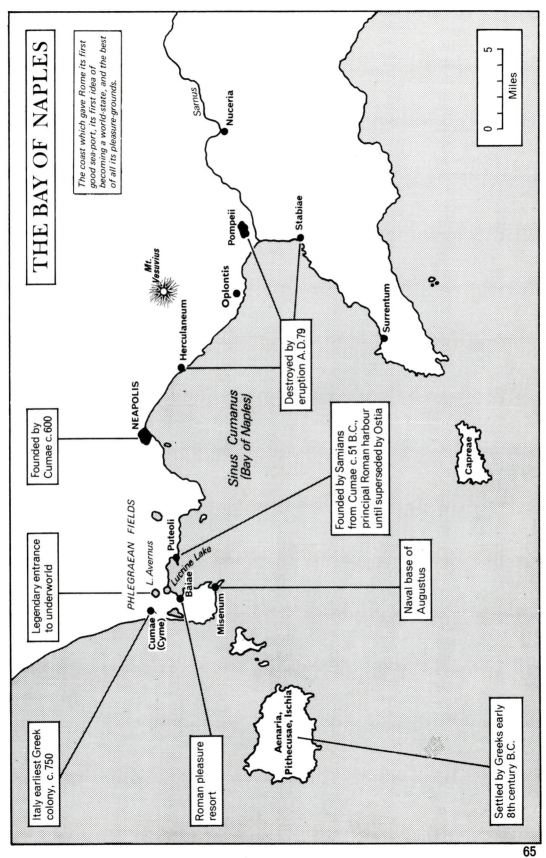

THE BAY OF NAPLES

The coast which gave Rome its first good sea-port, its first idea of becoming a world-state, and the best of all its pleasure-grounds.

Sarnus

Nuceria

Pompeii

Stabiae

Mt. *Vesuvius*

Oplontis

Herculaneum

Surrentum

NEAPOLIS

Founded by Cumae c. 600

Destroyed by eruption A.D. 79

Sinus Cumanus (Bay of Naples)

Founded by Samians from Cumae c. 51 B.C., principal Roman harbour until superseded by Ostia

PHLEGRAEAN FIELDS

Puteoli

L. Avernus

Lucrine Lake

Legendary entrance to underworld

Baiae

Misenum

Naval base of Augustus

Cumae (Cyme)

Caprea

Italy earliest Greek colony, c. 750

Roman pleasure resort

Aenaria, Pithecusae, Ischia

Settled by Greeks early 8th century B.C.

0   5

Miles

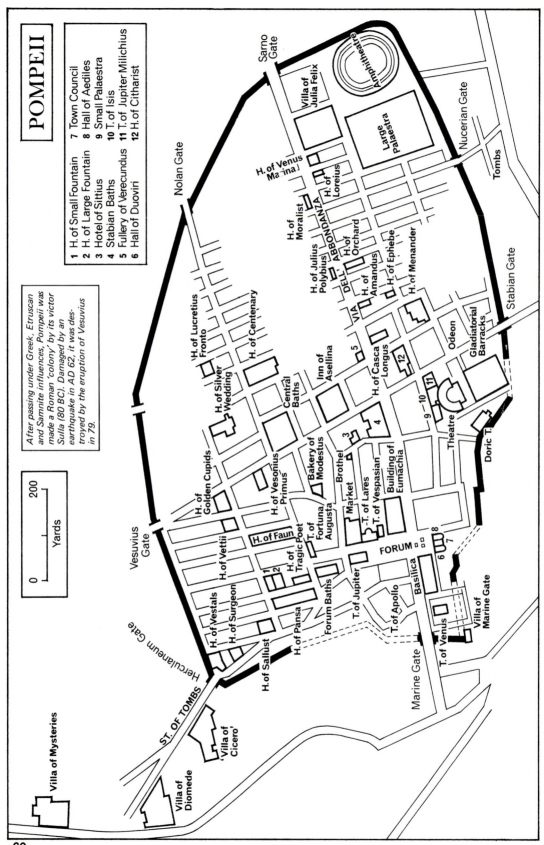

POMPEII

1 H. of Small Fountain
2 H. of Large Fountain
3 Hotel of Sittius
4 Stabian Baths
5 Fullery of Verecundus
6 Hall of Duoviri
7 Town Council
8 Hall of Aediles
9 Small Palaestra
10 T. of Isis
11 T. of Jupiter Milichius
12 H. of Citharist

After passing under Greek, Etruscan and Samnite influences, Pompeii was made a Roman 'colony' by its victor Sulla (80 BC). Damaged by an earthquake in AD 62, it was destroyed by the eruption of Vesuvius in 79.

Yards
0   200

Sarno Gate

Villa of Julia Felix

Amphitheatre

Nucerian Gate

Large Palaestra

Tombs

H. of Venus Marina

Nolan Gate

H. of Loreius

H. of Moralist

DELL' ABBONDANZA

H. of Orchard

H. of Julius Polybius

VIA

H. of Amandus

H. of Ephebe

H. of Menander

H. of Lucretius Fronto

H. of Centenary

Inn of Asellina

5

H. of Casca Longus

12

Stabian Gate

'H. of Silver Wedding

Central Baths

Odeon

9 – 10

11

Gladiatorial Barracks

H. of Golden Cupids

H. of Vesonius Primus

Bakery of Modestus

Brothel

3

4

Theatre

Doric T.

T. of Fortuna Augusta

Market

T. of Lares

T. of Vespasian

Building of Eumachia

Vesuvius Gate

H. of Vettii

H. of Faun

T. of Tragic Poet

1
2

FORUM

8

7

6

H. of Surgeon

H. of Vestals

H. of Pansa

Forum Baths

T. of Jupiter

Basilica

T. of Apollo

T. of Venus

Villa of Marine Gate

Marine Gate

H. of Sallust

Herculaneum Gate

ST. OF TOMBS

Villa of Mysteries

'Villa of Cicero'

Villa of Diomede

66

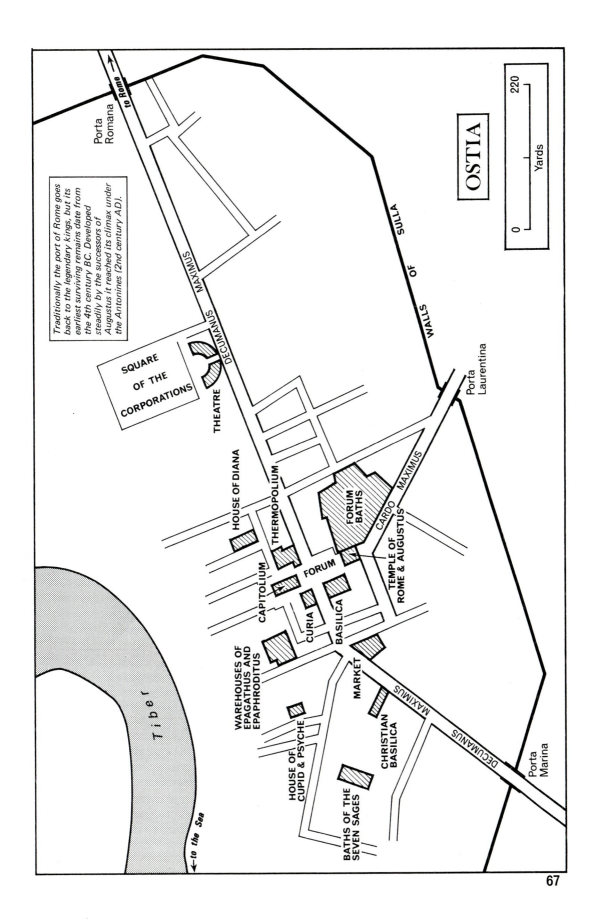

OSTIA

Traditionally the port of Rome goes back to the legendary kings, but its earliest surviving remains date from the 4th century BC. Developed steadily by the successors of Augustus it reached its climax under the Antonines (2nd century AD).

Porta Romana

to Rome

DECUMANUS MAXIMUS

SQUARE OF THE CORPORATIONS

THEATRE

HOUSE OF DIANA

THERMOPOLIUM

CAPITOLIUM

FORUM

CURIA

BASILICA

FORUM BATHS

CARDO MAXIMUS

TEMPLE OF ROME & AUGUSTUS

WALLS OF SULLA

Porta Laurentina

WAREHOUSES OF EPAGATHUS AND EPAPHRODITUS

MARKET

CHRISTIAN BASILICA

HOUSE OF CUPID & PSYCHE

BATHS OF THE SEVEN SAGES

DECUMANUS MAXIMUS

Porta Marina

Tiber

to the Sea

0 ———————— 220

Yards

67

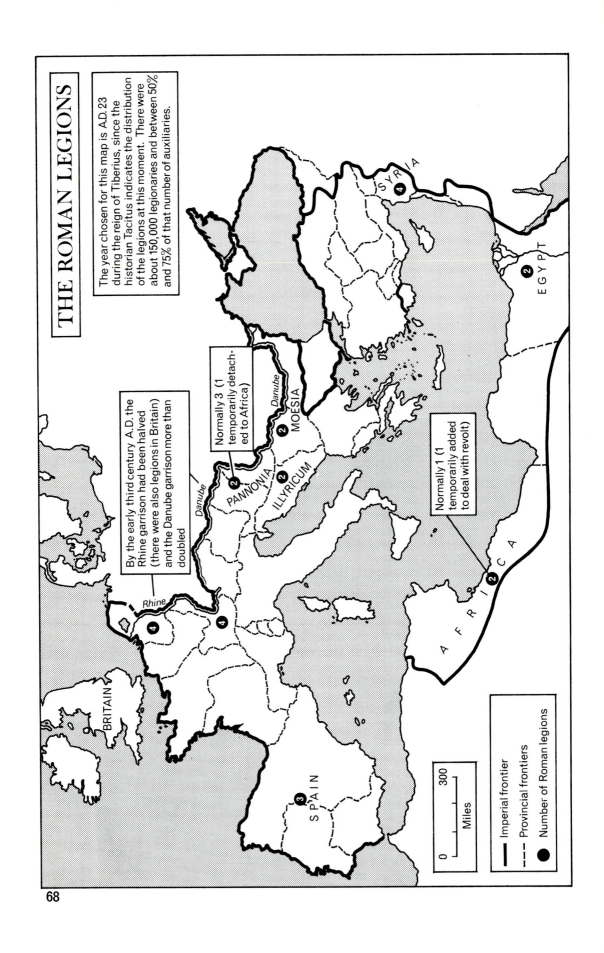

THE ROMAN LEGIONS

The year chosen for this map is A.D. 23 during the reign of Tiberius, since the historian Tacitus indicates the distribution of the legions at this moment. There were about 150,000 legionaries and between 50% and 75% of that number of auxiliaries.

Normally 3 (1 temporarily detached to Africa)

Normally 1 (1 temporarily added to deal with revolt)

By the early third century A.D. the Rhine garrison had been halved (there were also legions in Britain) and the Danube garrison more than doubled

Danube

Danube

MOESIA

PANNONIA

ILLYRICUM

Rhine

BRITAIN

SPAIN

AFRICA

SYRIA

EGYPT

Legend:
— Imperial frontier
--- Provincial frontiers
● Number of Roman legions

0   300
Miles

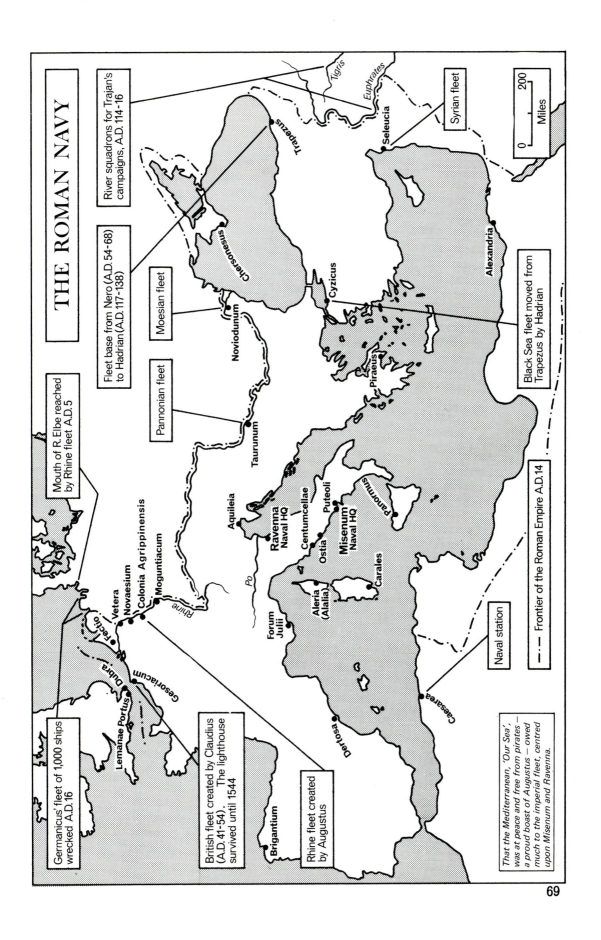

THE ROMAN NAVY

Germanicus' fleet of 1,000 ships wrecked A.D.16

Mouth of R. Elbe reached by Rhine fleet A.D.5

River squadrons for Trajan's campaigns, A.D. 114-16

Fleet base from Nero (A.D. 54-68) to Hadrian (A.D. 117-138)

Moesian fleet

Pannonian fleet

Syrian fleet

Black Sea fleet moved from Trapezus by Hadrian

British fleet created by Claudius (A.D. 41-54). The lighthouse survived until 1544

Rhine fleet created by Augustus

Naval station

— ·· — Frontier of the Roman Empire A.D.14

That the Mediterranean, 'Our Sea', was at peace and free from pirates — a proud boast of Augustus — owed much to the imperial fleet, centred upon Misenum and Ravenna.

Tigris

Euphrates

Seleucia

Alexandria

Trapezus

Chersonesus

Cyzicus

Noviodunum

Piraeus

Taurunum

Aquileia

Ravenna Naval HQ

Centumcellae

Puteoli

Ostia

Misenum Naval HQ

Pannonius

Carrales

Aleria (Alalia)

Forum Julii

Po

Rhine

Moguntiacum

Colonia Agrippinensis

Novaesium

Vetera

Gesoriacum

Dubra

Lemanae Portus

Gessio

Brigantium

Caesarea

Dertosa

0   200
Miles

BRITANNIA (AD 71)
(AD 59)
(AD 43-47)
Londinium

FREE GERMANY

LOWER GERMANY
Colonia Agrippinensis

Rhine
Moguntiacum

AGRI DECUMAT. (83)

LUGDUNENSIS

UPPER GERMANY

RHAETIA

NORICUM

Danube

PANNONIA

UPPER

LOWER

GALLIA

Lugdunum

AQUITANIA

NARBONENSIS

Aquileia

ILLYRICUM

Nemausus

Adriatic Sea

TARRACONENSIS

HISPANIA

Tarraco

I T A L I A

LUSITANIA

SARDINIA

Rome

BAETICA

Corduba

Gades

SICILY

Carthage

MAURETANIA (A.D.42)

A F R I C A

- - - Frontier of Roman Empire A.D. 14
- · - Frontier of Roman Empire A.D. 117
· · · · Province boundaries

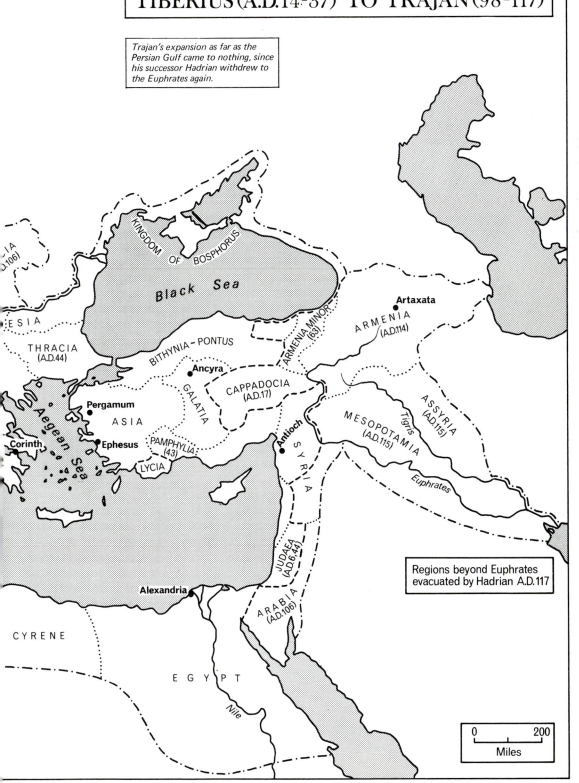

THE ROMAN EMPIRE FROM
TIBERIUS (A.D.14-37) TO TRAJAN (98-117)

Trajan's expansion as far as the Persian Gulf came to nothing, since his successor Hadrian withdrew to the Euphrates again.

KINGDOM OF BOSPHORUS

Black Sea

THRACIA (A.D.44)

ESIA

BITHYNIA – PONTUS

ARMENIA MINOR (63)

Artaxata

ARMENIA (A.D.114)

Ancyra

GALATIA

CAPPADOCIA (A.D.17)

ASSYRIA (A.D.115)

Tigris

MESOPOTAMIA (A.D.115)

Pergamum

ASIA

Corinth

Aegean Sea

Ephesus

PAMPHYLIA (43)

LYCIA

Antioch

S Y R I A

Euphrates

JUDAEA (A.D.6,44)

Regions beyond Euphrates evacuated by Hadrian A.D.117

Alexandria

ARABIA (A.D.106)

CYRENE

E G Y P T

Nile

0   200

Miles

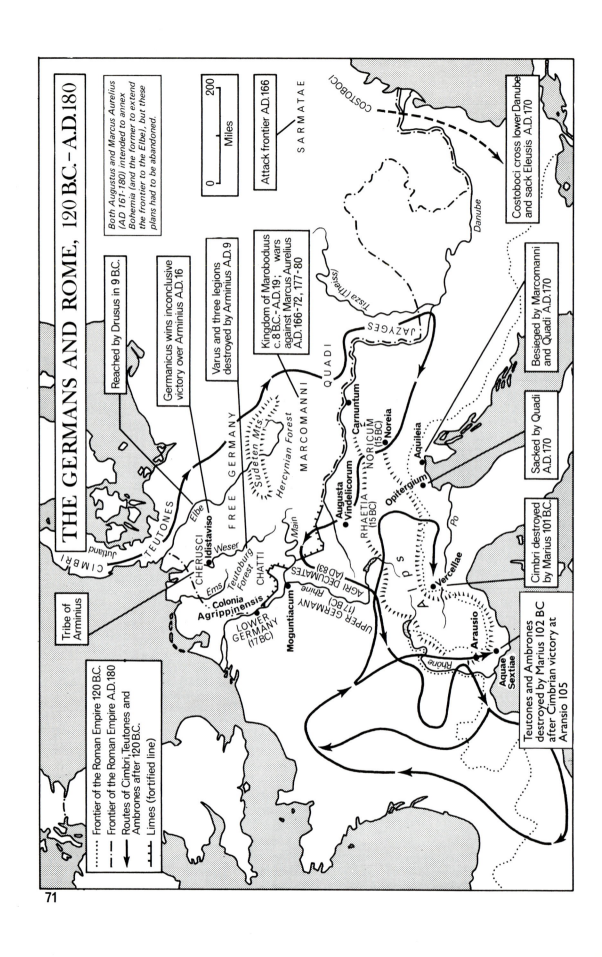

THE GERMANS AND ROME, 120 B.C.-A.D.180

Both Augustus and Marcus Aurelius (AD 161–180) intended to annex Bohemia (and the former to extend the frontier to the Elbe), but these plans had to be abandoned.

```
0          200
|—————————|
    Miles
```

Reached by Drusus in 9 B.C.

Germanicus wins inconclusive victory over Arminius A.D.16

Varus and three legions destroyed by Arminius A.D.9

Kingdom of Maroboduus c.8 B.C.–A.D.19; wars against Marcus Aurelius A.D.166–72, 177–80

Attack frontier A.D.166

Costoboci cross lower Danube and sack Eleusis A.D.170

Besieged by Marcomanni and Quadi A.D.170

Sacked by Quadi A.D.170

Cimbri destroyed by Marius 101 B.C.

Teutones and Ambrones destroyed by Marius 102 BC after Cimbrian victory at Aransio 105

Tribe of Arminius

.... Frontier of the Roman Empire 120 B.C.

—·— Frontier of the Roman Empire A.D.180

→ Routes of Cimbri, Teutones and Ambrones after 120 B.C.

⊥⊥⊥ Limes (fortified line)

SARMATAE

COSTOBOCI

Danube

Tisza (Theiss)

JAZYGES

QUADI

MARCOMANNI

Hercynian Forest

Sudeten Mts.

FREE GERMANY

CHERUSCI

Idistaviso

Weser

Elbe

Ems

Teutoburg Forest

CHATTI

Colonia Agrippinensis

LOWER GERMANY (17 BC)

Moguntiacum

Rhine

UPPER GERMANY (17 BC)

AGRI DECUMATES (AD 83)

Main

Augusta Vindelicorum

RHAETIA (15 BC)

NORICUM (15 BC)

Noreia

Carnuntum

Aquileia

Opitergium

A L P S

Po

Vercellae

Arausio

Rhone

Aquae Sextiae

TEUTONES

CIMBRI

Jutland

71

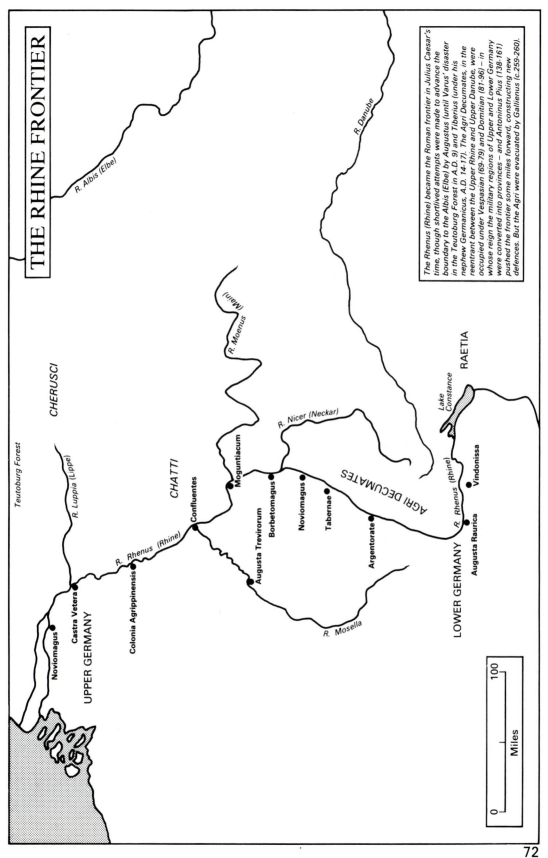

THE RHINE FRONTIER

R. Albis (Elbe)

R. Danube

CHERUSCI

Teutoburg Forest

R. Luppia (Lippe)

CHATTI

R. Rhenus (Rhine)

Confluentes

Moguntiacum

R. Moenus (Main)

R. Nicer (Neckar)

Borbetomagus

Noviomagus

Augusta Treviorum

Tabernae

AGRI DECUMATES

Argentorate

R. Mosella

Lake Constance

RAETIA

R. Rhenus (Rhine)

Vindonissa

LOWER GERMANY

R. Rhenus (Rhine)

Augusta Raurica

Noviomagus

Castra Vetera

Colonia Agrippinensis

UPPER GERMANY

The Rhenus (Rhine) became the Roman frontier in Julius Caesar's time, though shortlived attempts were made to advance the boundary to the Albis (Elbe) by Augustus (until Varus' disaster in the Teutoburg Forest in A.D. 9) and Tiberius (under his nephew Germanicus, A.D. 14-17). The Agri Decumates, in the reentrant between the Upper Rhine and Upper Danube, were occupied under Vespasian (69-79) and Domitian (81-96) – in whose reign the military regions of Upper and Lower Germany were converted into provinces – and Antoninus Pius (138-161) pushed the frontier some miles forward, constructing new defences. But the Agri were evacuated by Gallienus (c.259-260).

0   100
Miles

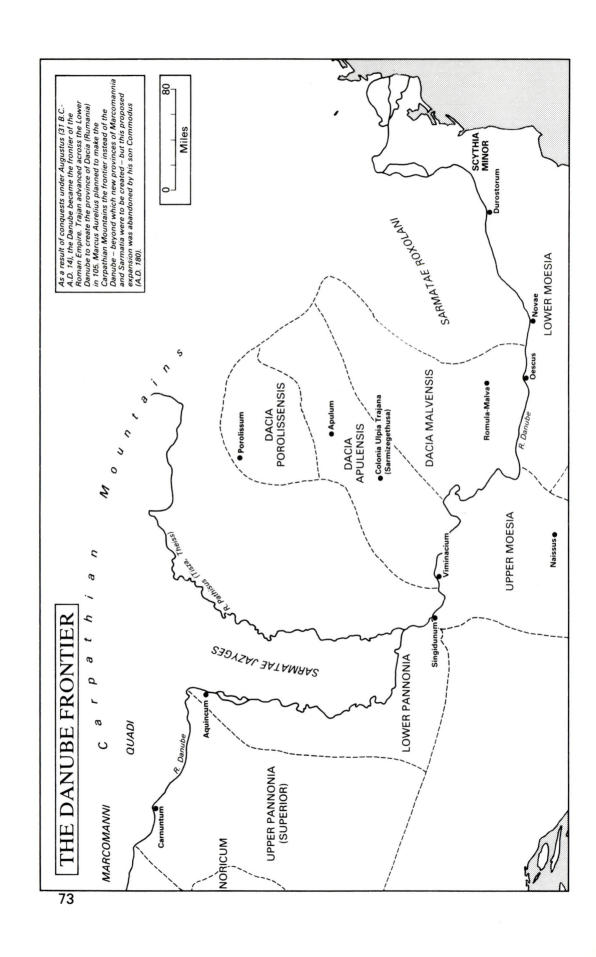

THE DANUBE FRONTIER

As a result of conquests under Augustus (31 B.C.–A.D. 14), the Danube became the frontier of the Roman Empire. Trajan advanced across the Lower Danube to create the province of Dacia (Rumania) in 105. Marcus Aurelius planned to make the Carpathian Mountains the frontier instead of the Danube – beyond which new provinces of Marcomannia and Sarmatia were to be created – but this proposed expansion was abandoned by his son Commodus (A.D. 180).

Miles
0   80

MARCOMANNI

C a r p a t h i a n   M o u n t a i n s

QUADI

NORICUM

R. Danube

UPPER PANNONIA (SUPERIOR)

● Carnuntum

● Aquincum

R. Pathisus (Tisza, Theiss)

SARMATAE JAZYGES

LOWER PANNONIA

DACIA POROLISSENSIS

● Porolissum

● Apulum

DACIA APULENSIS

● Colonia Ulpia Trajana (Sarmizegethusa)

DACIA MALVENSIS

● Singidunum

● Viminacium

UPPER MOESIA

● Naissus

Romula-Malva ●

R. Danube

SARMATAE ROXOLANI

Oescus ●

Novae ●

LOWER MOESIA

Durostorum ●

SCYTHIA MINOR

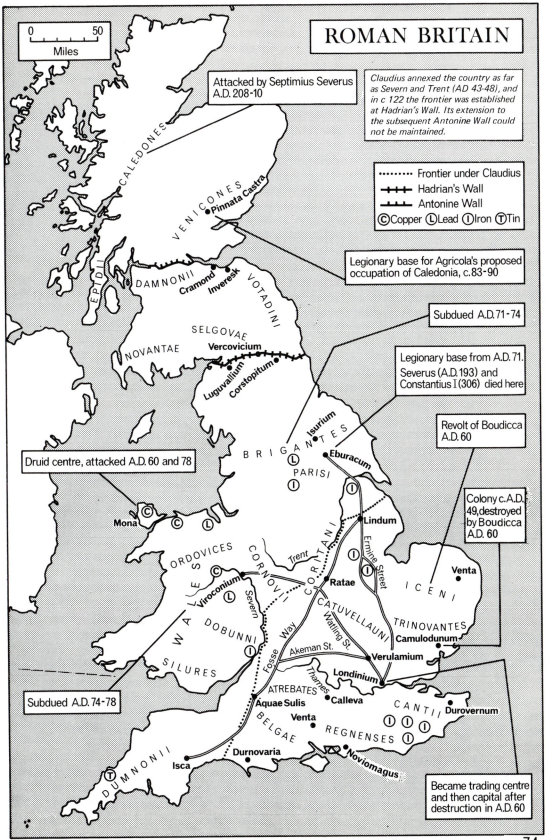

ROMAN BRITAIN

Attacked by Septimius Severus
A.D. 208-10

Claudius annexed the country as far
as Severn and Trent (AD 43-48), and
in c 122 the frontier was established
at Hadrian's Wall. Its extension to
the subsequent Antonine Wall could
not be maintained.

········· Frontier under Claudius
╈╈╈ Hadrian's Wall
╨╨ Antonine Wall
Ⓒ Copper Ⓛ Lead Ⓘ Iron Ⓣ Tin

Legionary base for Agricola's proposed
occupation of Caledonia, c.83-90

Subdued A.D. 71-74

Legionary base from A.D. 71.
Severus (A.D.193) and
Constantius I (306) died here

Revolt of Boudicca
A.D. 60

Druid centre, attacked A.D. 60 and 78

Colony c.A.D.
49, destroyed
by Boudicca
A.D. 60

Subdued A.D. 74-78

Became trading centre
and then capital after
destruction in A.D. 60

CALEDONES
EPIDII
VENICONES
Pinnata Castra
DAMNONII
Cramond **Inveresk**
VOTADINI
SELGOVAE
Vercovicium
NOVANTAE
Luguvallium **Corstopitum**
B R I G A N T E S
Isurium
PARISI
Ⓛ
Eburacum
Mona Ⓒ
Ⓒ Ⓛ
ORDOVICES
CORNOVII
Ⓘ
CORITANI
Ⓘ
Lindum
Trent
Ⓒ
Viroconium
Ⓛ
Severn
Ⓘ Ⓘ
Ermine Street
Ratae
Venta
I C E N I
WALES
DOBUNNI
Ⓘ
CATUVELLAUNI
Watling St.
TRINOVANTES
Camulodunum
SILURES
Fosse Way
Akeman St.
Verulamium
Thames
Londinium
ATREBATES
Calleva
C A N T I I
Aquae Sulis
Venta
Durovernum
BELGAE
REGNENSES
Ⓘ Ⓘ Ⓘ
Ⓘ Ⓘ
Durnovaria
Ⓘ
⊠
Noviomagus
Ⓣ
DUMNONII
Isca

0   50
Miles

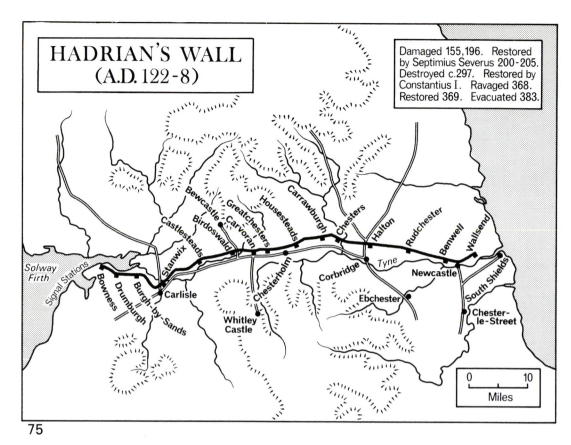

HADRIAN'S WALL
(A.D. 122-8)

Damaged 155,196. Restored by Septimius Severus 200-205. Destroyed c.297. Restored by Constantius I. Ravaged 368. Restored 369. Evacuated 383.

Bewcastle

Greatchesters

Housesteads

Carrawburgh

Chesters

Halton

Rudchester

Benwell

Wallsend

Castlesteads

Birdoswald

Carvoran

Stanwix

Chesterholm

Corbridge

Tyne

Newcastle

South Shields

Solway Firth

Signal Stations

Bowness

Drumburgh

Burgh-by-Sands

Carlisle

Whitley Castle

Ebchester

Chester-le-Street

0   10
Miles

75

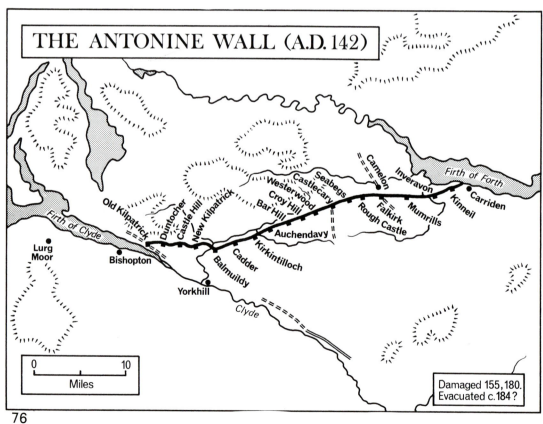

THE ANTONINE WALL (A.D. 142)

Camelon

Inveravon

Firth of Forth

Seabegs

Castlecary

Westerwood

Croy Hill

Bar Hill

Falkirk

Mumrills

Kinneil

Carriden

Old Kilpatrick

Duntocher

Castle Hill

New Kilpatrick

Rough Castle

Auchendavy

Firth of Clyde

Lurg Moor

Bishopton

Cadder

Kirkintilloch

Balmuildy

Yorkhill

Clyde

0   10
Miles

Damaged 155,180.
Evacuated c.184?

76

THE WORLD ACCORDING TO PTOLEMY, c. A.D.150

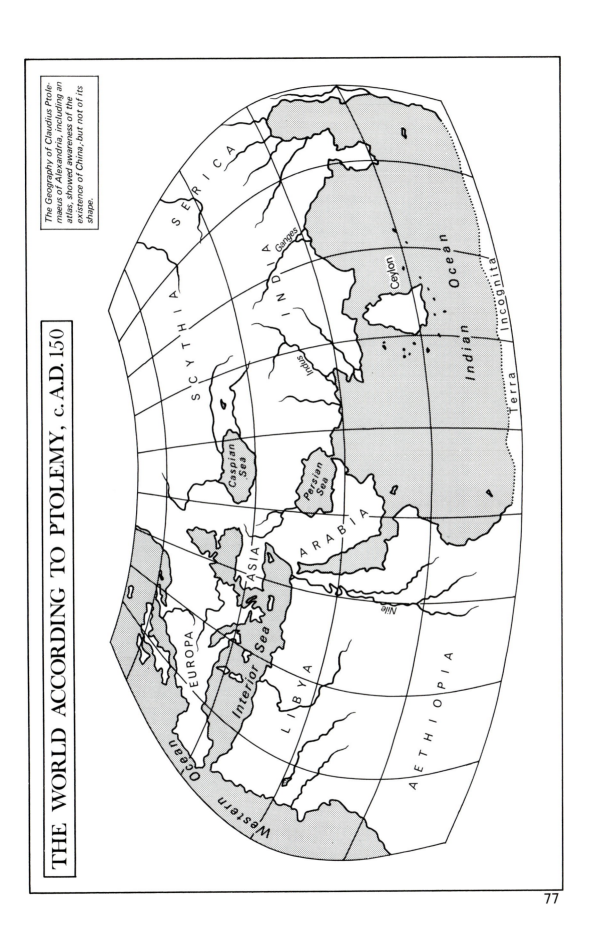

The Geography of Claudius Ptolemaeus of Alexandria, including an atlas, showed awareness of the existence of China, but not of its shape.

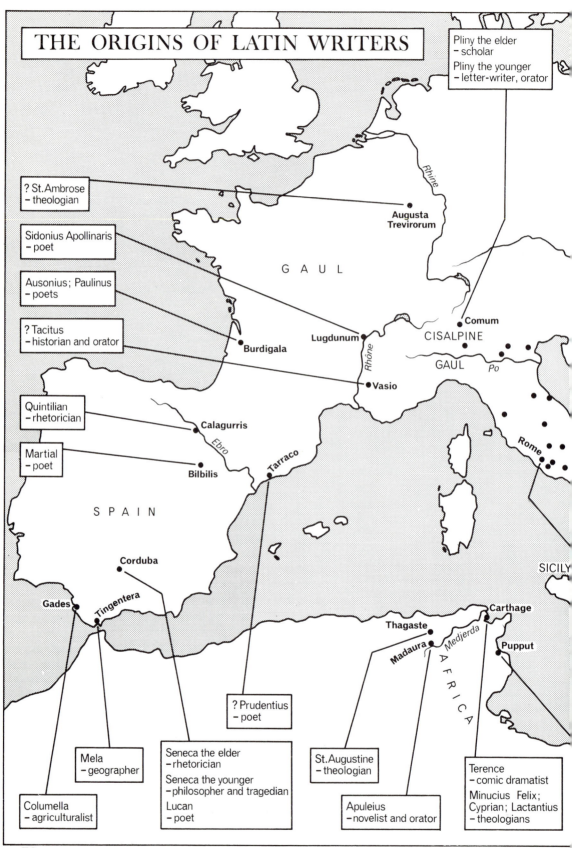

THE ORIGINS OF LATIN WRITERS

Pliny the elder
– scholar
Pliny the younger
– letter-writer, orator

? St.Ambrose
– theologian

Sidonius Apollinaris
– poet

Ausonius; Paulinus
– poets

? Tacitus
– historian and orator

Quintilian
– rhetorician

Martial
– poet

GAUL

Rhine

Comum

CISALPINE

Lugdunum

GAUL

Rhône

Po

Burdigala

Vasio

Augusta
Trevirorum

Calagurris

Ebro

Bilbilis

Tarraco

Rome

SPAIN

Corduba

SICILY

Gades

Tingentera

Carthage

Thagaste

Madaura

Medjerda

Pupput

AFRICA

? Prudentius
– poet

Mela
– geographer

Seneca the elder
– rhetorician

Seneca the younger
– philosopher and tragedian

Lucan
– poet

St.Augustine
– theologian

Terence
– comic dramatist

Minucius Felix;
Cyprian; Lactantius
– theologians

Columella
– agriculturalist

Apuleius
– novelist and orator

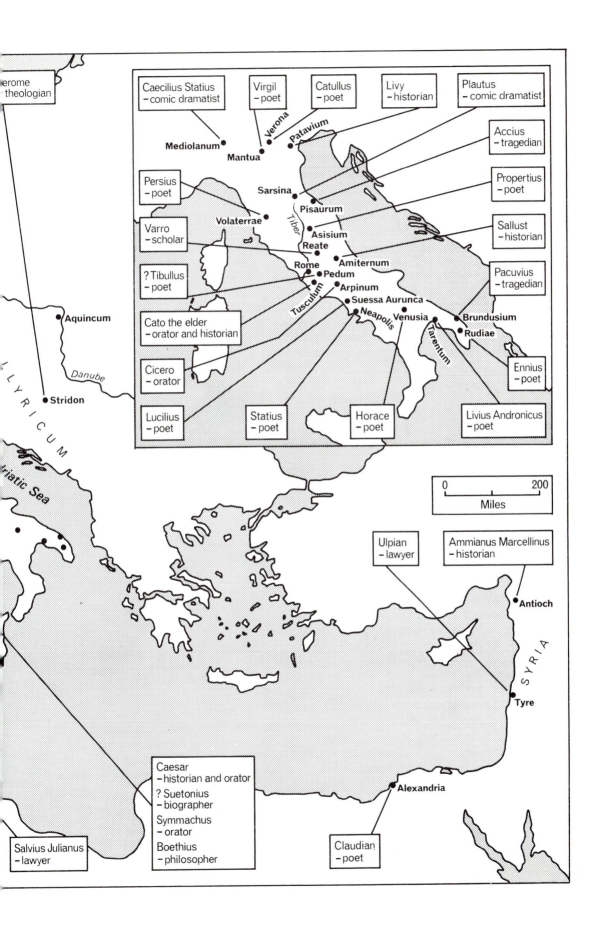

Jerome
– theologian

Caecilius Statius
– comic dramatist

Virgil
– poet

Catullus
– poet

Livy
– historian

Plautus
– comic dramatist

Accius
– tragedian

Propertius
– poet

Persius
– poet

Sallust
– historian

Varro
– scholar

?Tibullus
– poet

Pacuvius
– tragedian

Cato the elder
– orator and historian

Cicero
– orator

Ennius
– poet

Lucilius
– poet

Statius
– poet

Horace
– poet

Livius Andronicus
– poet

Ulpian
– lawyer

Ammianus Marcellinus
– historian

Caesar
– historian and orator
?Suetonius
– biographer
Symmachus
– orator
Boethius
– philosopher

Salvius Julianus
– lawyer

Claudian
– poet

Mediolanum
Mantua
Verona
Patavium
Sarsina
Pisaurum
Volaterrae
Asisium
Reate
Rome
Amiternum
Pedum
Arpinum
Tusculum
Suessa Aurunca
Neapolis
Venusia
Brundusium
Rudiae
Tarentum

Tiber

Aquincum
Stridon
Danube

ILLYRICUM
Adriatic Sea

SYRIA
Antioch
Tyre
Alexandria

0   200
Miles

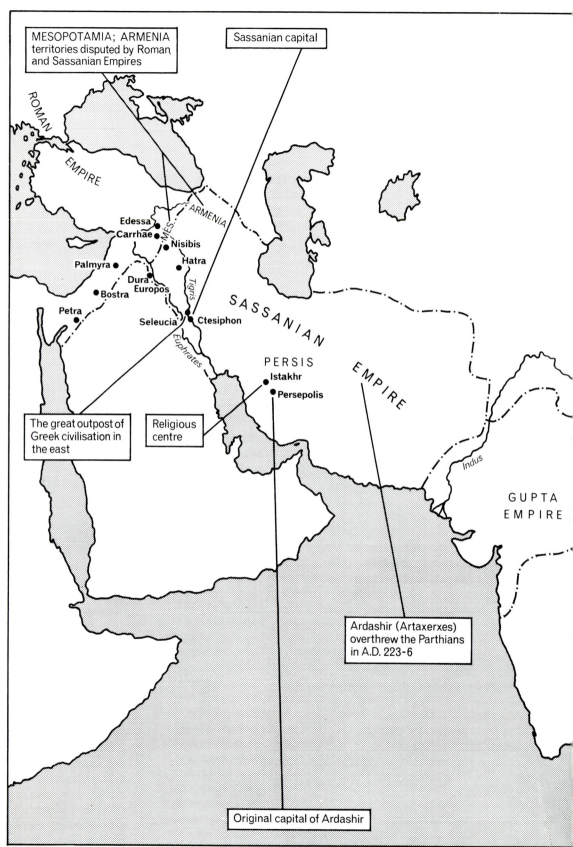

MESOPOTAMIA; ARMENIA
territories disputed by Roman
and Sassanian Empires

Sassanian capital

ROMAN

EMPIRE

ARMENIA

Edessa
Carrhae
MES.
Nisibis
Hatra
Palmyra
Dura
Europos
Tigris
Bostra
Petra
Seleucia
Ctesiphon

SASSANIAN

EMPIRE

PERSIS
Istakhr
Persepolis

Euphrates

The great outpost of
Greek civilisation in
the east

Religious
centre

Indus

GUPTA
EMPIRE

Ardashir (Artaxerxes)
overthrew the Parthians
in A.D. 223-6

Original capital of Ardashir

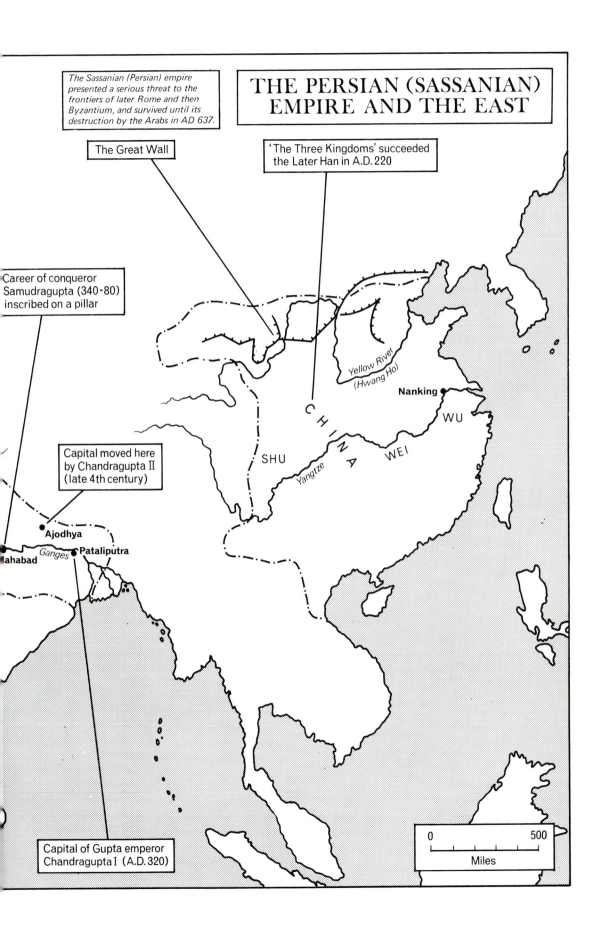

THE PERSIAN (SASSANIAN) EMPIRE AND THE EAST

The Sassanian (Persian) empire presented a serious threat to the frontiers of later Rome and then Byzantium, and survived until its destruction by the Arabs in AD 637.

The Great Wall

'The Three Kingdoms' succeeded the Later Han in A.D. 220

Career of conqueror Samudragupta (340-80) inscribed on a pillar

Capital moved here by Chandragupta II (late 4th century)

Yellow River (Hwang Ho)

Nanking

C H I N A

WU

SHU

WEI

Yangtze

Ajodhya

Ganges **Pataliputra**

ahabad

Capital of Gupta emperor Chandragupta I (A.D. 320)

0   500

Miles

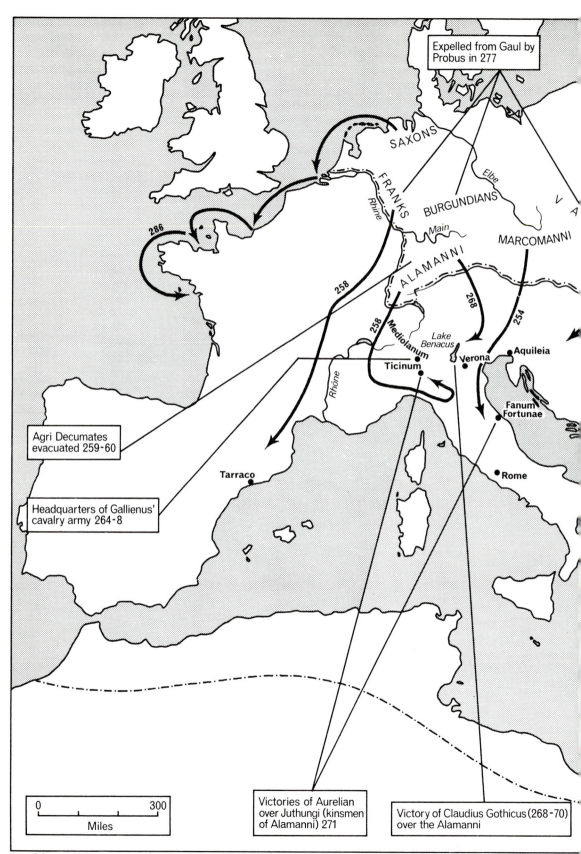

Expelled from Gaul by
Probus in 277

SAXONS

FRANKS

BURGUNDIANS

Elbe

MARCOMANNI

286

Rhine

Main

A L A M A N N I

258

258

Mediolanum

*Lake
Benacus*

268

254

Rhône

Ticinum

Verona

Aquileia

Agri Decumates
evacuated 259-60

Fanum
Fortunae

Headquarters of Gallienus'
cavalry army 264-8

Tarraco

Rome

Victories of Aurelian
over Juthungi (kinsmen
of Alamanni) 271

Victory of Claudius Gothicus (268-70)
over the Alamanni

0   300

Miles

GERMAN INVASIONS IN THE THIRD CENTURY A.D.

Evacuated c.271

First crossed the Danube under Severus Alexander (222-35

From the 230s until the 260s the Germans burst over the frontiers with ever increasing force, but then the dissolution of the empire was prevented by Gallienus, Claudius II Gothicus, Aurelian and Probus.

King lends fleet to raiders 254

Decius fell to Goths 251

Overrun by Goths 256

Victory of Gallienus over Goths 268

Captured by Goths from Decius (249-51)

Sacked by Goths in 253

Dnieper

Dniester

EAST GOTHS

HERULI

Cimmerian Bosphorus

Panticapaeum

A L S

quincum

DACIA

Danube

WEST GOTHS

Abrittus

264

269

Marcianopolis

Black Sea

Trapezus

SASSANIAN

EMPIRE

Naïssus

Philippopolis

Byzantium

Chalcedon

BITHYNIA

Thessalonica

Pessinus

Ephesus

Sparta

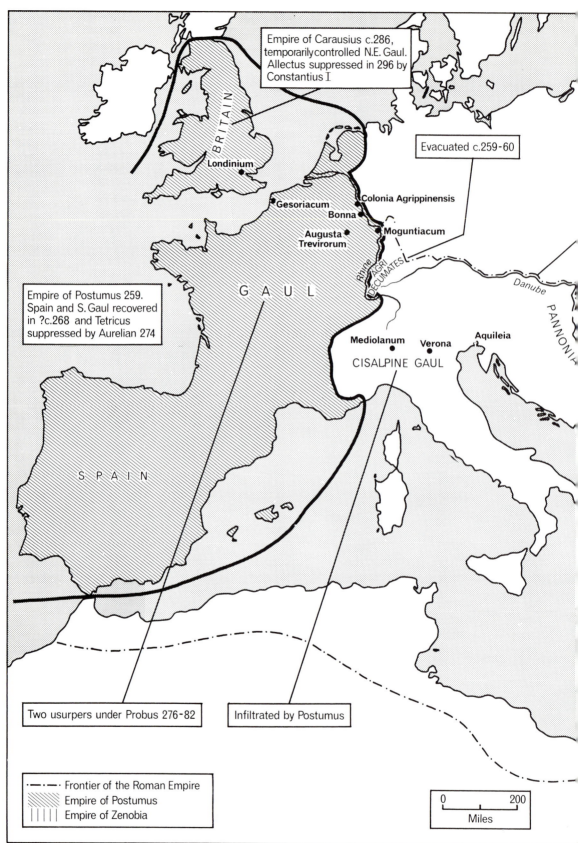

Empire of Carausius c.286, temporarily controlled N.E. Gaul. Allectus suppressed in 296 by Constantius I

Evacuated c.259-60

Empire of Postumus 259. Spain and S. Gaul recovered in ?c.268 and Tetricus suppressed by Aurelian 274

BRITAIN

Londinium

Gesoriacum

Colonia Agrippinensis

Bonna

Augusta Trevirorum

Moguntiacum

Rhine

AGRI DECUMATES

Danube

PANNONIA

GAUL

Mediolanum

Verona

Aquileia

CISALPINE GAUL

SPAIN

Two usurpers under Probus 276-82

Infiltrated by Postumus

Frontier of the Roman Empire
Empire of Postumus
Empire of Zenobia

0   200
Miles

81

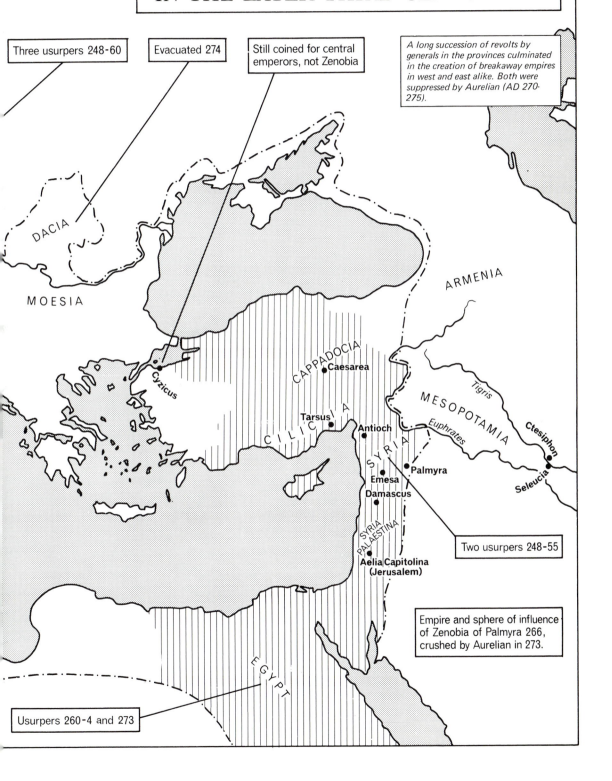

THE BREAKDOWN AND RECOVERY
OF THE ROMAN EMPIRE
IN THE LATER THIRD CENTURY A.D.

Three usurpers 248-60

Evacuated 274

Still coined for central
emperors, not Zenobia

*A long succession of revolts by
generals in the provinces culminated
in the creation of breakaway empires
in west and east alike. Both were
suppressed by Aurelian (AD 270-
275).*

DACIA

MOESIA

ARMENIA

CAPPADOCIA
●Caesarea

Cyzicus

Tigris

MESOPOTAMIA

Ctesiphon

Tarsus
C I L I C I A

●Antioch

Euphrates

S Y R I A

Seleucia

Emesa

●Palmyra

Damascus

SYRIA
PALAESTINA

Two usurpers 248-55

Aelia Capitolina
(Jerusalem)

Empire and sphere of influence
of Zenobia of Palmyra 266,
crushed by Aurelian in 273.

E G Y P T

Usurpers 260-4 and 273

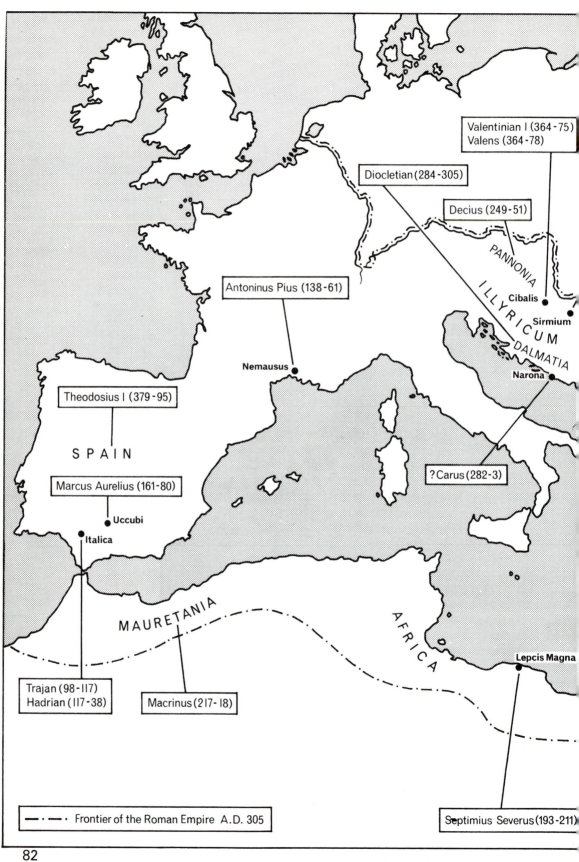

Valentinian I (364-75)
Valens (364-78)

Diocletian (284-305)

Decius (249-51)

PANNONIA

ILLYRICUM

Cibalis

Sirmium

DALMATIA

Antoninus Pius (138-61)

Narona

Nemausus

Theodosius I (379-95)

SPAIN

?Carus (282-3)

Marcus Aurelius (161-80)

Uccubi

Italica

MAURETANIA

AFRICA

Lepcis Magna

Trajan (98-117)
Hadrian (117-38)

Macrinus (217-18)

— · — Frontier of the Roman Empire A.D. 305

Septimius Severus (193-211)

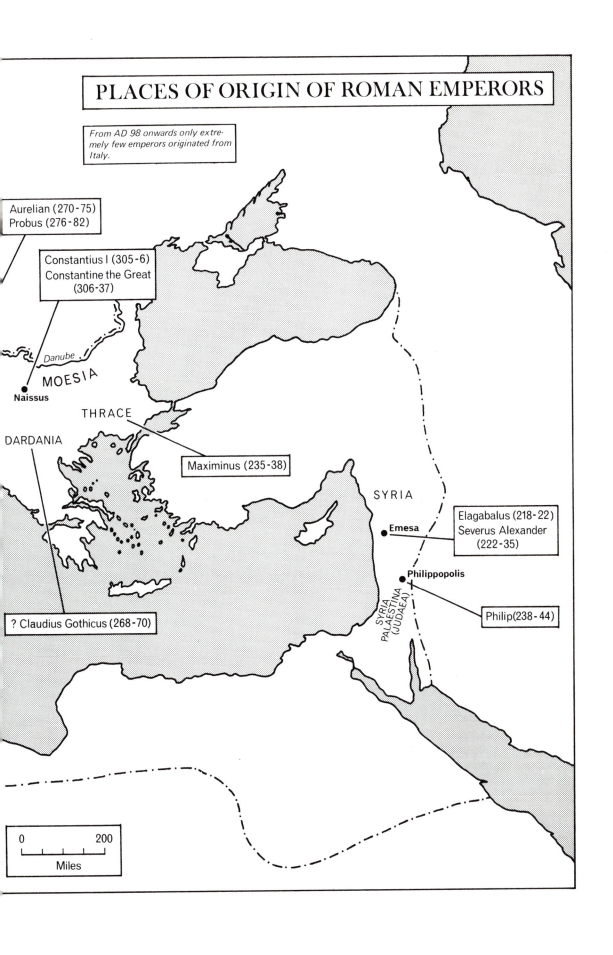

PLACES OF ORIGIN OF ROMAN EMPERORS

From AD 98 onwards only extremely few emperors originated from Italy.

Aurelian (270-75)
Probus (276-82)

Constantius I (305-6)
Constantine the Great
(306-37)

Danube

MOESIA

Naissus

THRACE

DARDANIA

Maximinus (235-38)

SYRIA

Emesa

Elagabalus (218-22)
Severus Alexander
(222-35)

Philippopolis

SYRIA
PALAESTINA
(JUDAEA)

Philip(238-44)

? Claudius Gothicus (268-70)

0   200
Miles

GERMANIA

Colonia

Rhine

Regina

Aquincum

PANNONIA

Mursa

Lutetia

Genabum

Vesontio

Alps

Tergeste

Ravenna

DALMATIA

GAUL

Genua

ITALY

Burdigala

Pyrenees

Tolosa

Massilia

APULIA

Rome

CALABR

CAMPANIA

SPAIN

SARDINIA

Caralis

Panormus

Corduba

Jews deported from
Rome by Tiberius
A.D. 14 - 37

SICILY

Gades

Carthage

Melita

Volubilis

Atlas Mountains

SAHARA

Oea

| 0 | | | | 250 |

Miles

■ Areas of widespread Jewish settlement
● Towns with large Jewish communities

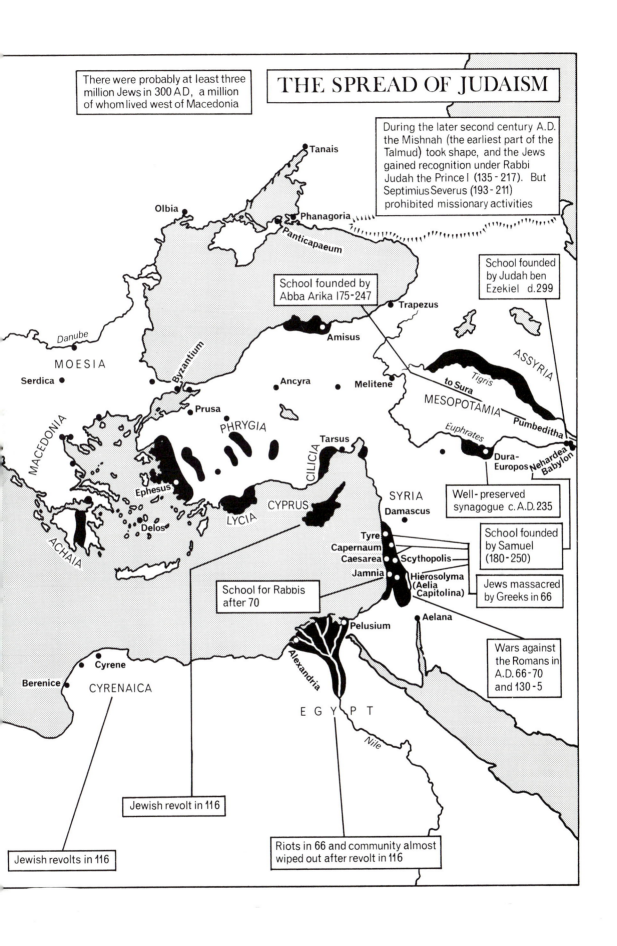

THE SPREAD OF JUDAISM

There were probably at least three million Jews in 300 A.D., a million of whom lived west of Macedonia

During the later second century A.D. the Mishnah (the earliest part of the Talmud) took shape, and the Jews gained recognition under Rabbi Judah the Prince I (135 - 217). But Septimius Severus (193 - 211) prohibited missionary activities

School founded by Judah ben Ezekiel d.299

School founded by Abba Arika 175-247

Tanais

Olbia

Phanagoria

Panticapaeum

Trapezus

Amisus

Danube

MOESIA

Byzantium

ASSYRIA

Tigris

to Sura

Serdica

Ancyra

Melitene

MESOPOTAMIA

Pumbeditha

Prusa

PHRYGIA

Euphrates

Tarsus

Babylon

MACEDONIA

CILICIA

Dura-Europos

Nehardea

Ephesus

CYPRUS

SYRIA

Well-preserved synagogue c. A.D. 235

Delos

LYCIA

Damascus

ACHAIA

Tyre

Capernaum

Caesarea

Scythopolis

School founded by Samuel (180 - 250)

Jamnia

Hierosolyma (Aelia Capitolina)

Jews massacred by Greeks in 66

School for Rabbis after 70

Aelana

Pelusium

Wars against the Romans in A.D. 66 - 70 and 130 - 5

Alexandria

Cyrene

Berenice

CYRENAICA

E G Y P T

Nile

Jewish revolt in 116

Riots in 66 and community almost wiped out after revolt in 116

Jewish revolts in 116

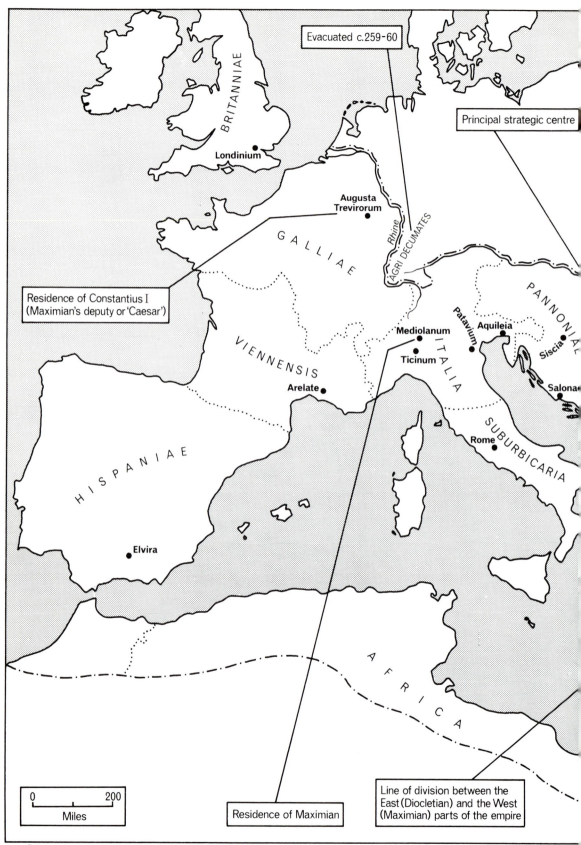

Evacuated c.259-60

Principal strategic centre

Residence of Constantius I
(Maximian's deputy or 'Caesar')

BRITANNIAE

Londinium

Augusta
Trevirorum

Rhine

AGRI DECUMATES

GALLIAE

PANNONIAE

VIENNENSIS

Mediolanum

Patavium

Aquileia

Siscia

Ticinum

ITALIA

Salonae

Arelate

SUBURBICARIA

Rome

HISPANIAE

Elvira

AFRICA

0   200
Miles

Residence of Maximian

Line of division between the
East (Diocletian) and the West
(Maximian) parts of the empire

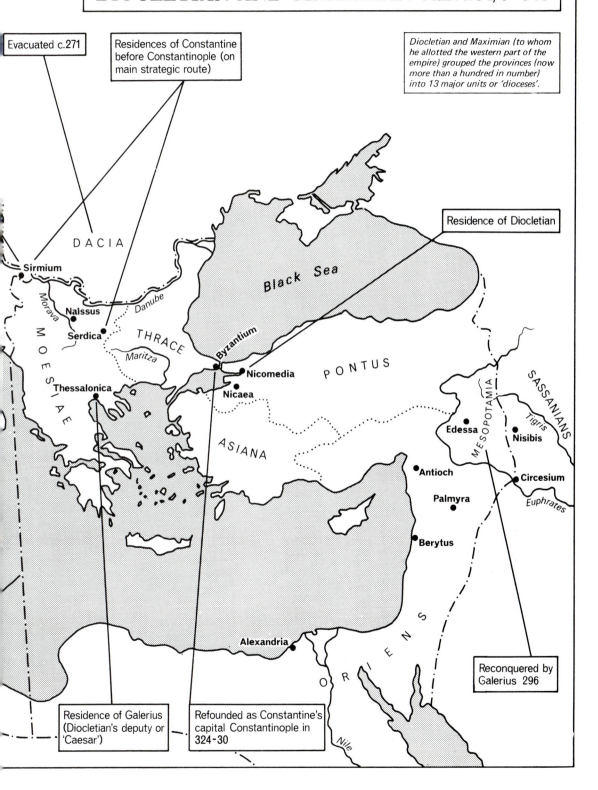

THE ROMAN EMPIRE UNDER DIOCLETIAN AND MAXIMIAN A.D. 284/6-305

Evacuated c.271

Residences of Constantine before Constantinople (on main strategic route)

Diocletian and Maximian (to whom he allotted the western part of the empire) grouped the provinces (now more than a hundred in number) into 13 major units or 'dioceses'.

Residence of Diocletian

DACIA

Black Sea

Sirmium

Morava

Naissus

Danube

Serdica

THRACE

Maritza

MOESIAE

Byzantium

PONTUS

Thessalonica

Nicomedia

Nicaea

ASIANA

MESOPOTAMIA

SASSANIANS

Edessa

Nisibis

Tigris

Antioch

Circesium

Palmyra

Euphrates

Berytus

O R I E N S

Alexandria

Reconquered by Galerius 296

Residence of Galerius (Diocletian's deputy or 'Caesar')

Refounded as Constantine's capital Constantinople in 324-30

Nile

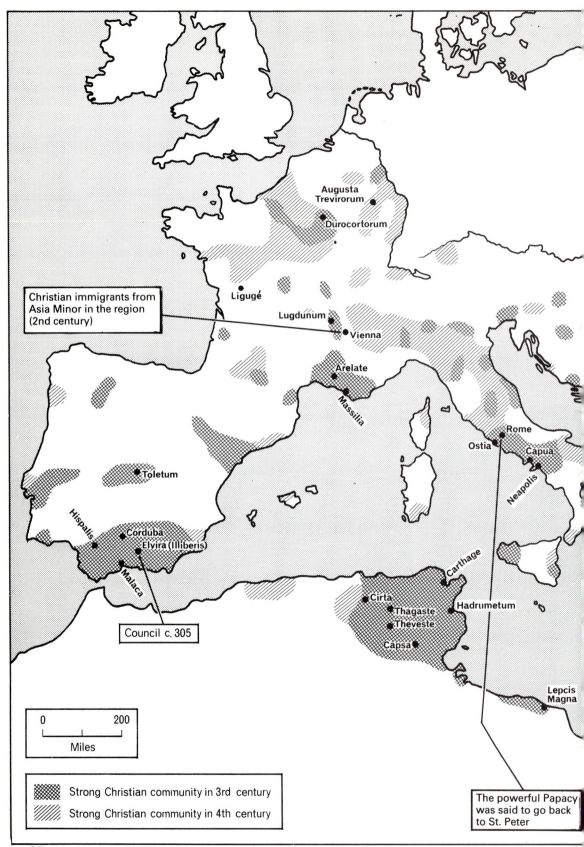

Christian immigrants from
Asia Minor in the region
(2nd century)

Augusta
Trevirorum

Durocortorum

Ligugé

Lugdunum
Vienna

Arelate

Massilia

Rome
Ostia
Capua

Neapolis

Toletum

Hispalis

Corduba
Elvira (Illiberis)

Malaca

Council c. 305

Carthage

Cirta
Thagaste
Theveste

Hadrumetum

Capsa

Lepcis
Magna

The powerful Papacy
was said to go back
to St. Peter

0   200
Miles

Strong Christian community in 3rd century

Strong Christian community in 4th century

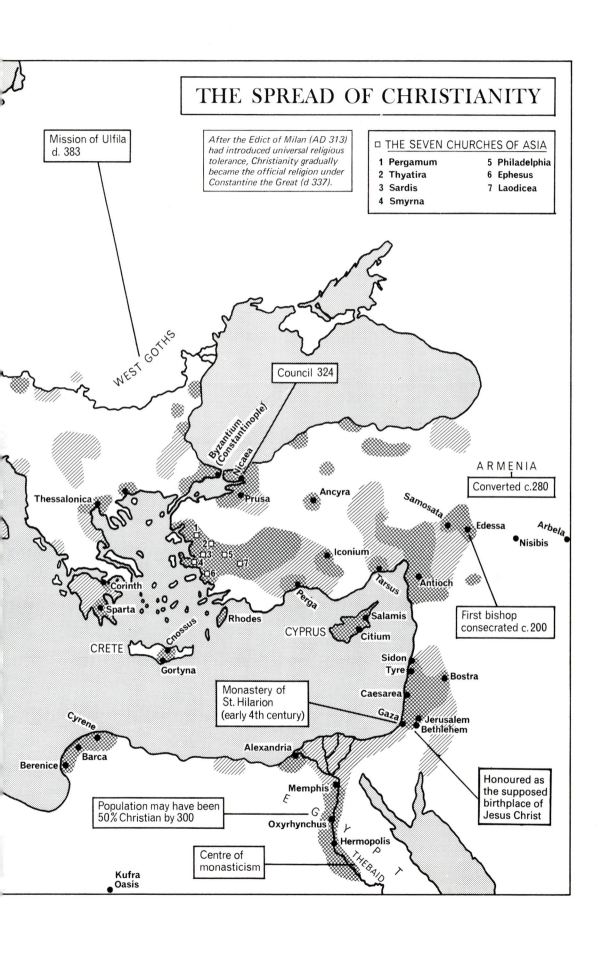

THE SPREAD OF CHRISTIANITY

Mission of Ulfila
d. 383

*After the Edict of Milan (AD 313)
had introduced universal religious
tolerance, Christianity gradually
became the official religion under
Constantine the Great (d 337).*

☐ THE SEVEN CHURCHES OF ASIA

1 Pergamum   **5** Philadelphia
2 Thyatira   **6** Ephesus
3 Sardis   **7** Laodicea
4 Smyrna

WEST GOTHS

Council 324

Byzantium
(Constantinople)
Nicaea

ARMENIA
Converted c.280

Thessalonica

Ancyra

Samosata

●Prusa

Edessa

Arbela
●

Nisibis

Iconium

Corinth

Perga

Tarsus

Antioch

First bishop
consecrated c.200

Sparta

Rhodes

Salamis

CYPRUS

Citium

Cnossus

CRETE

Sidon
Tyre

Bostra

Gortyna

Caesarea

Monastery of
St. Hilarion
(early 4th century)

Gaza

Jerusalem
Bethlehem

Cyrene

Honoured as
the supposed
birthplace of
Jesus Christ

Berenice

Barca

Alexandria

Memphis

E

Population may have been
50% Christian by 300

G

Oxyrhynchus

Y

Hermopolis

P

Centre of
monasticism

THEBAID

T

Kufra
Oasis

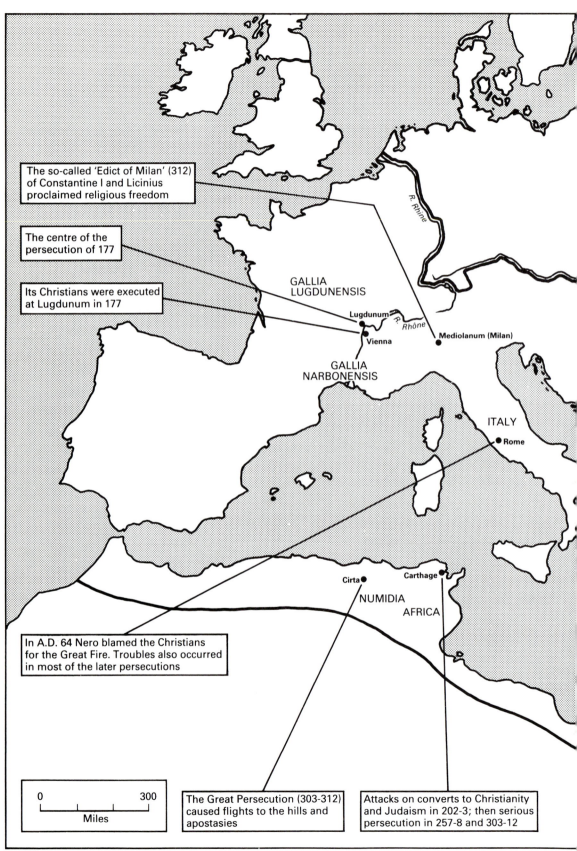

The so-called 'Edict of Milan' (312) of Constantine I and Licinius proclaimed religious freedom

The centre of the persecution of 177

Its Christians were executed at Lugdunum in 177

GALLIA LUGDUNENSIS

R. Rhine

Lugdunum

R. Rhône

Vienna

Mediolanum (Milan)

GALLIA NARBONENSIS

ITALY

Rome

Cirta

Carthage

NUMIDIA

AFRICA

In A.D. 64 Nero blamed the Christians for the Great Fire. Troubles also occurred in most of the later persecutions

0   300
Miles

The Great Persecution (303-312) caused flights to the hills and apostasies

Attacks on converts to Christianity and Judaism in 202-3; then serious persecution in 257-8 and 303-12

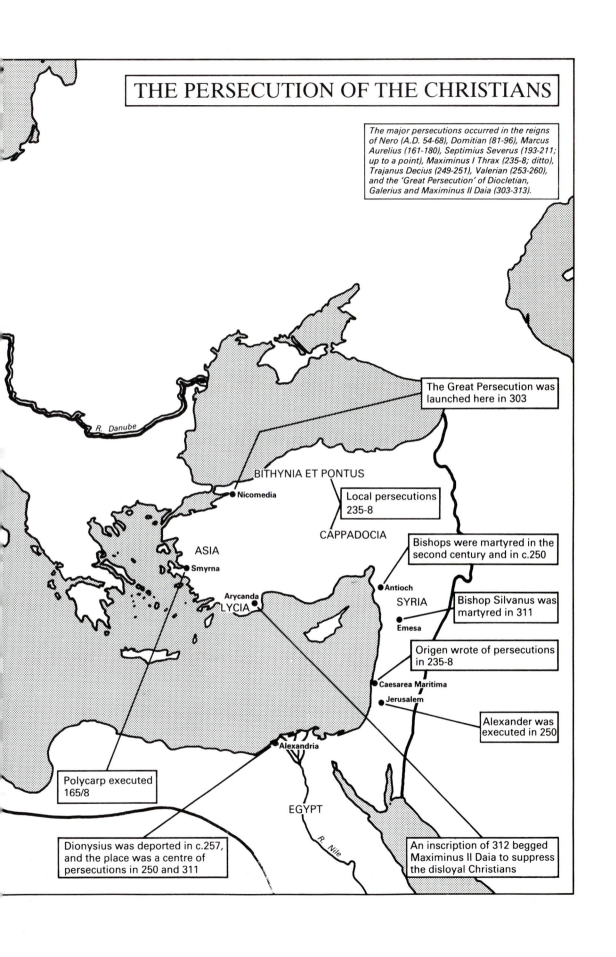

THE PERSECUTION OF THE CHRISTIANS

The major persecutions occurred in the reigns of Nero (A.D. 54-68), Domitian (81-96), Marcus Aurelius (161-180), Septimius Severus (193-211; up to a point), Maximinus I Thrax (235-8; ditto), Trajanus Decius (249-251), Valerian (253-260), and the 'Great Persecution' of Diocletian, Galerius and Maximinus II Daia (303-313).

The Great Persecution was launched here in 303

R. Danube

BITHYNIA ET PONTUS

● Nicomedia

Local persecutions 235-8

CAPPADOCIA

Bishops were martyred in the second century and in c.250

ASIA

● Smyrna

Arycanda ●
LYCIA

● Antioch

SYRIA

Bishop Silvanus was martyred in 311

● Emesa

Origen wrote of persecutions in 235-8

● Caesarea Maritima
● Jerusalem

Alexander was executed in 250

Polycarp executed 165/8

● Alexandria

EGYPT

R. Nile

Dionysius was deported in c.257, and the place was a centre of persecutions in 250 and 311

An inscription of 312 begged Maximinus II Daia to suppress the disloyal Christians

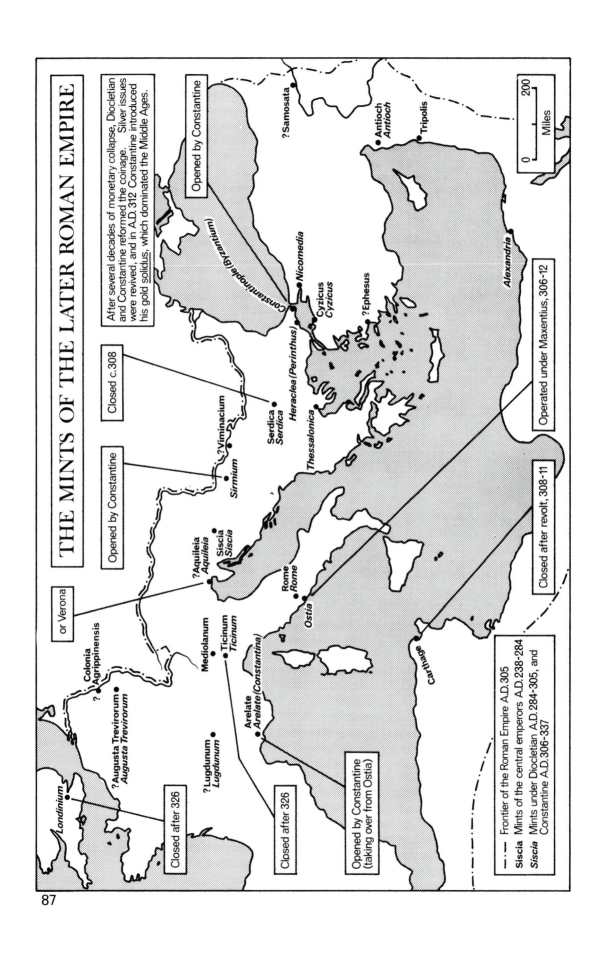

THE MINTS OF THE LATER ROMAN EMPIRE

After several decades of monetary collapse, Diocletian and Constantine reformed the coinage. Silver issues were revived, and in A.D. 312 Constantine introduced his gold solidus, which dominated the Middle Ages.

Opened by Constantine

Closed c.308

Opened by Constantine

or Verona

Closed after 326

Closed after 326

Opened by Constantine (taking over from Ostia)

Operated under Maxentius, 306-12

Closed after revolt, 308-11

Colonia Agrippinensis

?

?Augusta Trevirorum
Augusta Trevirorum

?Lugdunum
Lugdunum

Mediolanum

Ticinum
Ticinum

Arelate
Arelate (Constantina)

Aquileia
Aquileia

Siscia
Siscia

Rome
Rome

Ostia

Carthage

?Viminacium

Sirmium

Serdica
Serdica

Heraclea (Perinthus)

Thessalonica

Constantinople (Byzantium)

Nicomedia

Cyzicus
Cyzicus

?Ephesus

?Samosata

Antioch
Antioch

Tripolis

Alexandria

Londinium

0   200
Miles

- · - · — Frontier of the Roman Empire A.D.305
- **Siscia** Mints of the central emperors A.D.238-284
- *Siscia* Mints under Diocletian A.D.284-305, and Constantine A.D.306-337

87

THE ROMAN EMPIRE IN A.D. 395

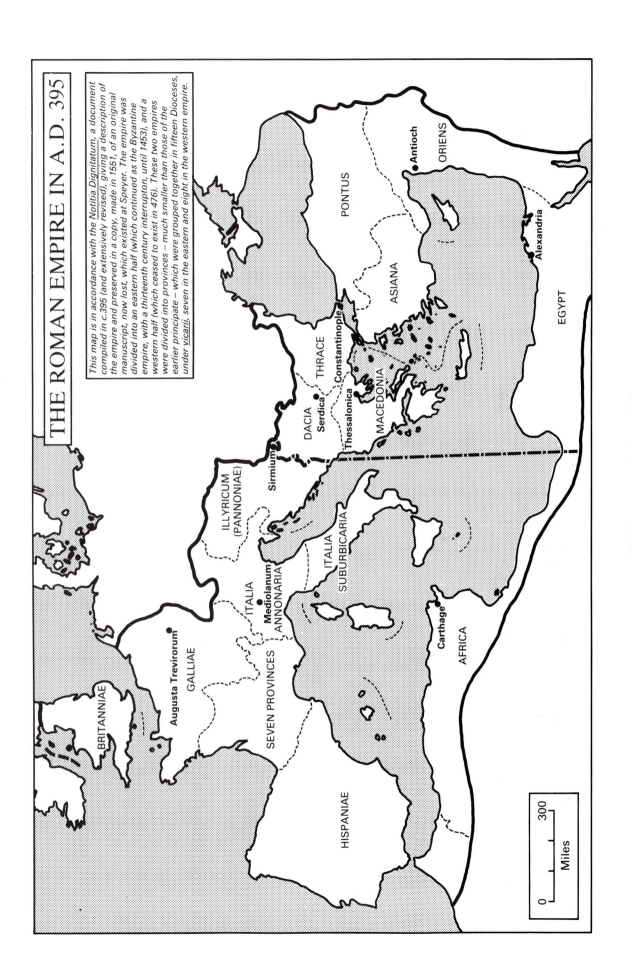

This map is in accordance with the Notitia Dignitatum, a document compiled in c.395 (and extensively revised), giving a description of the empire and preserved in a copy, made in 1551, of an original manuscript, now lost, which existed at Speyer. The empire was divided into an eastern half (which continued as the Byzantine empire, with a thirteenth century interrupton, until 1453), and a western half (which ceased to exist in 476). These two empires were divided into provinces – much smaller than those of the earlier principate – which were grouped together in fifteen Dioceses, under <u>vicarii</u>, seven in the eastern and eight in the western empire.

BRITANNIAE

GALLIAE

Augusta Trevirorum

SEVEN PROVINCES

ITALIA

Mediolanum
ITALIA ANNONARIA

HISPANIAE

ITALIA SUBURBICARIA

Carthage

AFRICA

ILLYRICUM (PANNONIAE)

Sirmium

DACIA

Serdica

THRACE

Thessalonica

Constantinople

MACEDONIA

PONTUS

ASIANA

ORIENS

Antioch

Alexandria

EGYPT

0   300

Miles

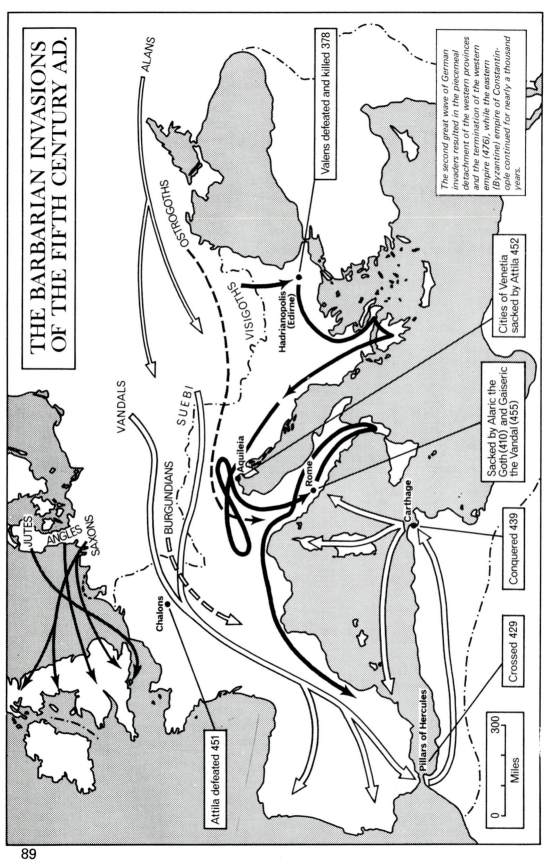

THE BARBARIAN INVASIONS OF THE FIFTH CENTURY A.D.

ALANS

OSTROGOTHS

VISIGOTHS

Valens defeated and killed 378

Hadrianopolis (Edirne)

The second great wave of German invaders resulted in the piecemeal detachment of the western provinces and the termination of the western empire (476), while the eastern (Byzantine) empire of Constantinople continued for nearly a thousand years.

Cities of Venetia sacked by Attila 452

VANDALS

SUEBI

BURGUNDIANS

Aquileia

Rome

Sacked by Alaric the Goth (410) and Gaiseric the Vandal (455)

Carthage

Conquered 439

JUTES

ANGLES

SAXONS

Chalons

Attila defeated 451

Crossed 429

Pillars of Hercules

300

Miles

0

89

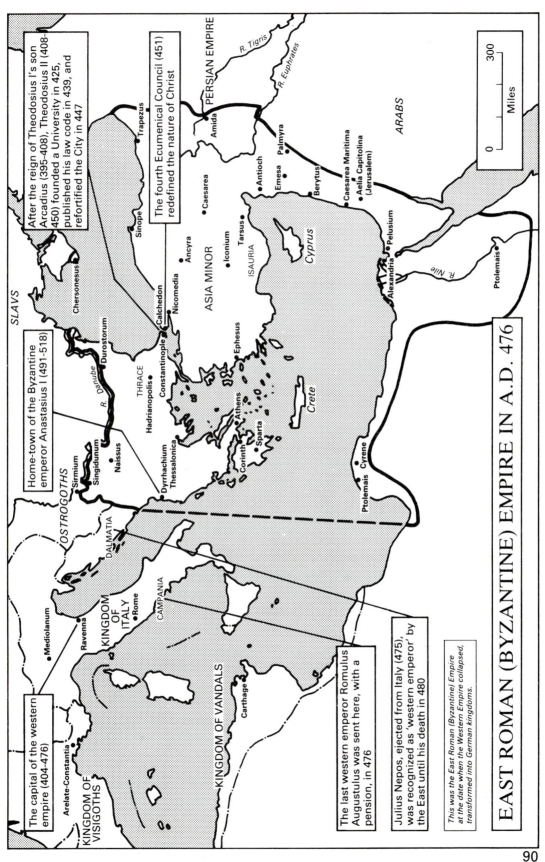

EAST ROMAN (BYZANTINE) EMPIRE IN A.D. 476

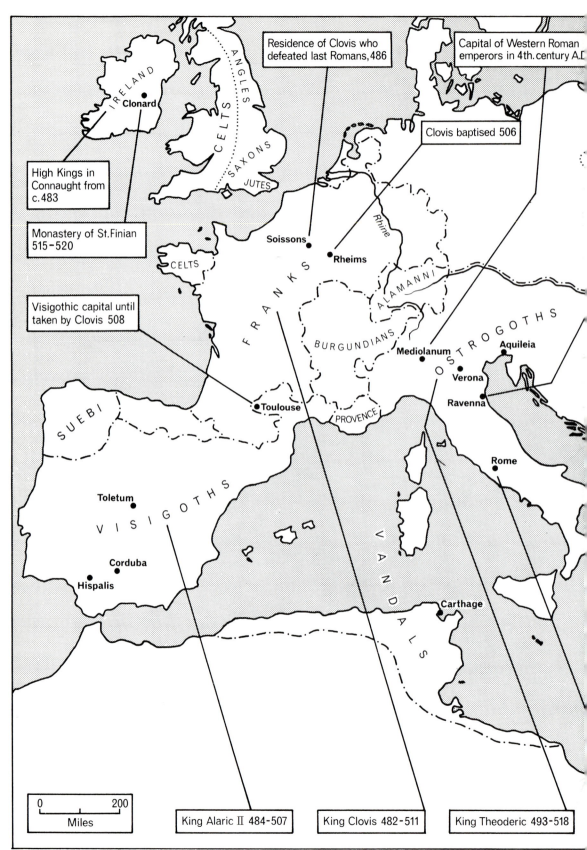

Residence of Clovis who
defeated last Romans, 486

Capital of Western Roman
emperors in 4th. century A.D

Clovis baptised 506

High Kings in
Connaught from
c.483

Monastery of St.Finian
515-520

Visigothic capital until
taken by Clovis 508

IRELAND

Clonard

ANGLES

CELTS

SAXONS

JUTES

CELTS

F R A N K S

Soissons

Rheims

Rhine

ALAMANNI

BURGUNDIANS

Mediolanum

O S T R O G O T H S

Aquileia

Verona

Ravenna

PROVENCE

Toulouse

S U E B I

V I S I G O T H S

Toletum

Corduba

Hispalis

V A N D A L S

Rome

Carthage

0   200

Miles

King Alaric II 484-507

King Clovis 482-511

King Theoderic 493-518

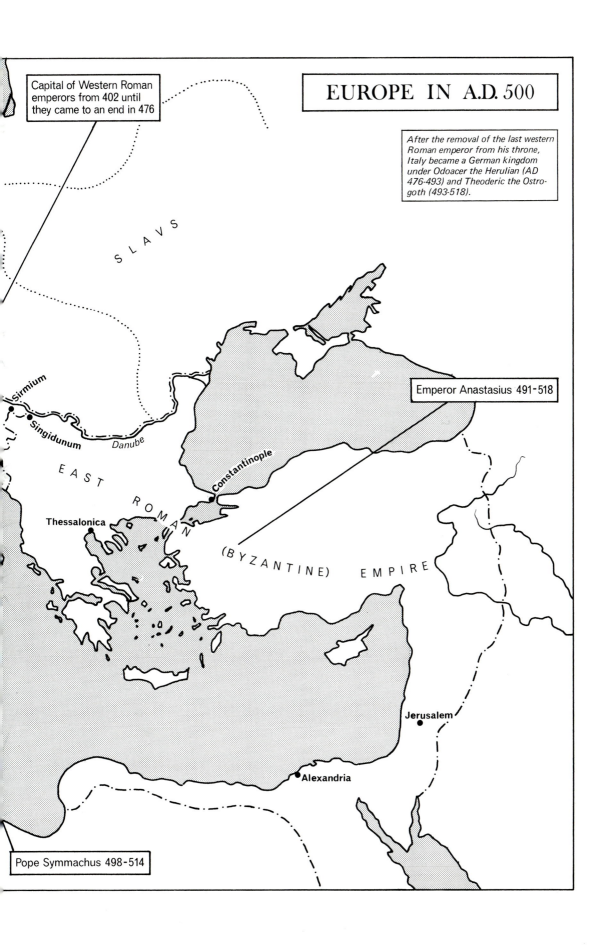

Capital of Western Roman emperors from 402 until they came to an end in 476

After the removal of the last western Roman emperor from his throne, Italy became a German kingdom under Odoacer the Herulian (AD 476-493) and Theoderic the Ostrogoth (493-518).

SLAVS

Sirmium

Singidunum

Danube

EAST

ROMAN

Constantinople

Emperor Anastasius 491-518

Thessalonica

(BYZANTINE) EMPIRE

Jerusalem

Alexandria

Pope Symmachus 498-514

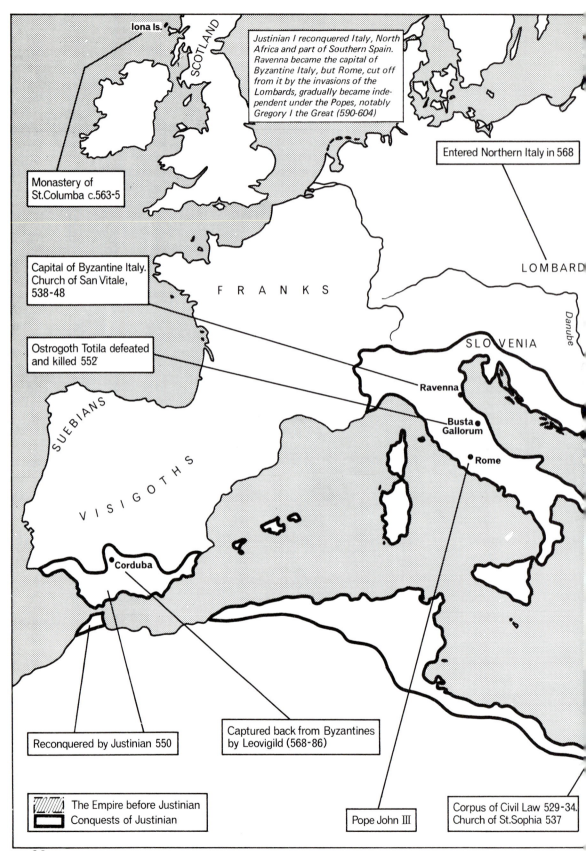

Iona Is.

SCOTLAND

Justinian I reconquered Italy, North
Africa and part of Southern Spain.
Ravenna became the capital of
Byzantine Italy, but Rome, cut off
from it by the invasions of the
Lombards, gradually became inde-
pendent under the Popes, notably
Gregory I the Great (590-604)

Entered Northern Italy in 568

Monastery of
St.Columba c.563-5

Capital of Byzantine Italy.
Church of San Vitale,
538-48

F R A N K S

LOMBARD

Danube

S L O VENIA

Ostrogoth Totila defeated
and killed 552

Ravenna

Busta
Gallorum

SUEBIANS

Rome

V I S I G O T H S

Corduba

Reconquered by Justinian 550

Captured back from Byzantines
by Leovigild (568-86)

The Empire before Justinian
Conquests of Justinian

Pope John III

Corpus of Civil Law 529-34.
Church of St.Sophia 537

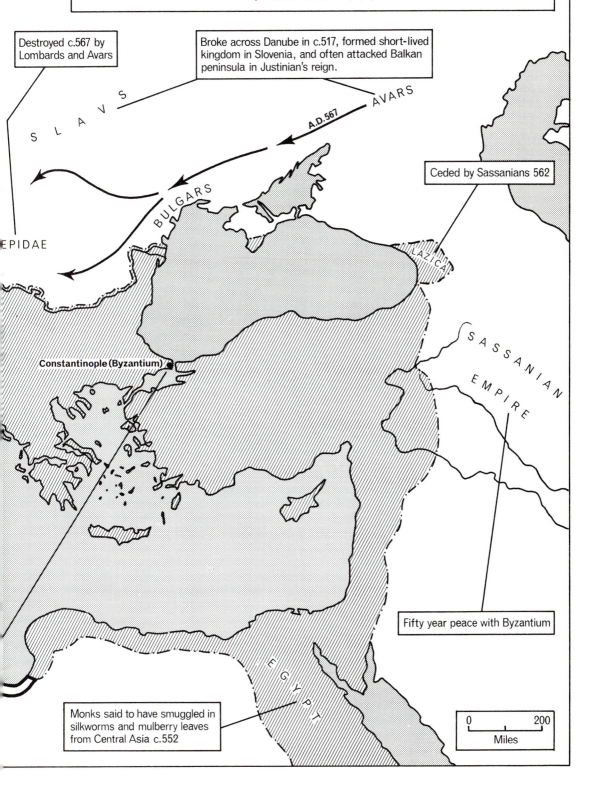

THE BYZANTINE EMPIRE OF JUSTINIAN I
(A.D. 527-65)

Destroyed c.567 by
Lombards and Avars

Broke across Danube in c.517, formed short-lived
kingdom in Slovenia, and often attacked Balkan
peninsula in Justinian's reign.

S L A V S

AVARS

A.D. 567

Ceded by Sassanians 562

B U L G A R S

EPIDAE

LAZICA

S A S S A N I A N

Constantinople (Byzantium)

E M P I R E

Fifty year peace with Byzantium

E G Y P T

Monks said to have smuggled in
silkworms and mulberry leaves
from Central Asia c.552

0   200

Miles

Index of Place Names[1]

Modern names are given in brackets

[1] I have sometimes sacrificed consistency of spelling to convenience and tradition.